The CURSE of the GOLDEN MONKEY

Starring

VON DOOGAN and...

WRITE YOUR NAME HERE!

DEAR *DARING PUZZLER*,

THANK YOU FOR JOINING ME
ON MY LATEST ESCAPADE:

The *CURSE of the GOLDEN MONKEY*

THIS *THRILLING ADVENTURE* IS CHOCK-FULL
OF MIND-BENDING *CHALLENGES* AND *PUZZLES*
THAT WILL TEST YOUR WITS TO THE *LIMIT!*

THERE'S SOME *VERY USEFUL INFORMATION*
OPPOSITE, AND A *LAST-MINUTE CHECKLIST*
OVER THE PAGE TO MAKE SURE YOU HAVE
EVERYTHING YOU NEED TO OVERCOME
THE *DANGEROUS PERILS*
THAT LIE AHEAD.

SO WHAT ARE YOU WAITING FOR?
LET'S GET STARTED!

Von Doogan

HOW THE BOOK WORKS

THIS BIT TELLS YOU THE PUZZLE **NAME** AND **NUMBER**.

THIS TELLS YOU HOW **TRICKY** THE PUZZLE IS!

PUZZLE No. 38

THE LAST WORDS

IMPOSSIBILITY LEVEL:

DOOGAN THINKS THE ADVENTURE'S OVER, WHEN HE SUDDENLY SPOTS SOMETHING...

HMM ... IF I ADD TWO WORDS TO THE DANGER KIT LINK, IT LOOKS LIKE I MIGHT UNLOCK A HIDDEN MESSAGE!

PERHAPS THESE SCRAPS OF PAPER HOLD THE KEY TO THE PROBLEM...?

FOLLOW THE STORY IN THE COMIC PANELS.

...S THE SCRAPS...

SEARCH THE PAGES FOR CLUES – THEY COULD BE ANYWHERE!

MPLET

VENT

URE ED AD CO

THIS BIT TELLS YOU WHAT YOU'LL NEED TO DO TO **SOLVE** THE PUZZLE.

CHALLENGE ONE!

WHAT ARE THE TWO WORDS DOOGAN IS LOOKING FOR?

CHALLENGE TWO!

WHAT SHOULD HE DO WITH THE WORDS WHEN HE HAS THEM?

THIS BIT TELLS YOU HOW **FAR** YOU ARE THROUGH THE ADVENTURE!

ADVENTURE PROGRESS *101%*

RIGHT! SO NOW YOU KNOW HOW THE BOOK WORKS, IT'S TIME TO CHECK OUR *EQUIPMENT* TO MAKE SURE WE HAVE EVERYTHING...

★★★ EQUIPMENT CHECKLIST ★★★

KEEN EYES AND A *SHARP BRAIN* ARE ALL THAT'S REQUIRED FOR MOST OF THE PUZZLES IN THIS BOOK. *HOWEVER*, THERE ARE A FEW CHALLENGES FOR WHICH YOU'LL ALSO NEED THE FOLLOWING:

★ A PENCIL
★ SOME SCRAP PAPER
★ A PAIR OF SCISSORS
★ A MIRROR

NEED HELP? THERE ARE **EXTRA CLUES** ON PAGE 42

STILL STUCK?! **SOLUTIONS** ON PAGE 44

FINALLY, THERE ARE SEVERAL *SPECIAL PUZZLES* WHICH WILL INSTRUCT YOU TO USE *ITEMS* FROM

DOOGAN'S DANGER KIT
★★★★★★★★ SEE PAGE 47 ★★★★★★★★★

GOT ALL THAT? THEN YOU'RE *READY!* OUR ADVENTURE BEGINS ON A SUNNY THURSDAY MORNING, WITH A *KNOCK* AT THE DOOR...

THE NINE LOCKS

WELCOME, FRIENDS, TO THE HOME OF THAT DARING YOUNG ADVENTURER – *VON DOOGAN!* THIS UNUSUAL ABODE IS *CRAMMED* TO THE *CLOISTERS* WITH AN INCONCEIVABLY *COLOSSAL* COLLECTION OF *CURIOSITIES*, PROTECTED BY A *VERY SPECIAL* SECURITY SYSTEM! HOWEVER, AT THIS *PRECISE* MOMENT, THE POSTMAN HAS ARRIVED WITH AN *IMPORTANT PACKAGE* FOR OUR HERO, AND IT SEEMS THAT DOOGAN'S FORGOTTEN EXACTLY *HOW* THE LOCKS WORK...!

CHALLENGE ONE!

THERE ARE *NINE LETTERED DOOR LOCKS*, WHICH MUST BE OPENED IN A *SPECIFIC* ORDER. DOOGAN HAS A SET OF *NOTES* TO HELP HIM (SEE *BELOW LEFT*) BUT THEY'RE A BIT JUMBLED UP. USING THE NOTES, AND A BIT OF DEDUCTION, *CAN YOU FIGURE OUT THE ORDER IN WHICH THE LOCKS SHOULD BE UNLOCKED, FROM FIRST TO LAST?*

THE SEVENTH LOCK TO BE UNLOCKED IS LOCK H • LOCK D CAN ONLY BE UNLOCKED DIRECTLY AFTER LOCK F • THE FOURTH LOCK TO BE UNLOCKED IS LOCK B • LOCK A MUST BE UNLOCKED BETWEEN LOCK H AND LOCK E • LOCK G CAN ONLY BE UNLOCKED DIRECTLY BEFORE LOCK B • LOCK C MUST BE UNLOCKED AFTER LOCK I, WHICH IS THE FIFTH LOCK TO BE UNLOCKED • LOCK F IS THE FIRST LOCK TO BE UNLOCKED •

CHALLENGE TWO!

GOT THE LOCK ORDER SORTED? *GOOD!* NOW, TRACE THE *WIRES* FROM EACH OF THE *LOCKS* TO EACH OF THE NUMBERED *SWITCHES*. IN WHAT ORDER SHOULD DOOGAN FLIP THE SWITCHES?

ADVENTURE PROGRESS 3%

PUZZLE No. 4 — THE DISHONEST DIRECTIONS

THE BOMBZILLA *ROARS* BACK INTO LIFE! DOOGAN PUMPS THE GAS PEDAL, SPINS THE WHEELS, AND THE BIG MACHINE *BUMPS* AND *SKIDS* OUT ONTO THE STREET. ITS DESTINATION...

SOUTHSIDE DOCKS →

I NEED TO MOVE *FAST* IF I'M TO REACH JAKE IN TIME, AND I'VE *NO IDEA* WHERE *PIER 19* IS! AH, THESE THREE GENTS UP AHEAD MAY BE ABLE TO GIVE ME *DIRECTIONS!*

DOOGAN LISTENS TO *INSTRUCTIONS* FROM THE *THREE STRANGERS* (SEE BELOW) BUT REALISES THAT ONLY *ONE* OF THEM HAS GIVEN HIM THE CORRECT DIRECTIONS.

THE CHALLENGE!

LOOKING AT THE MAP AND *ALL THREE* SETS OF DIRECTIONS, CAN YOU ANSWER THE QUESTIONS BELOW?
1. WHICH PIER IS PIER 19?
2. *WHO* TELLS YOU WHERE IT IS?
3. WHO IS *DELIBERATELY* LYING?

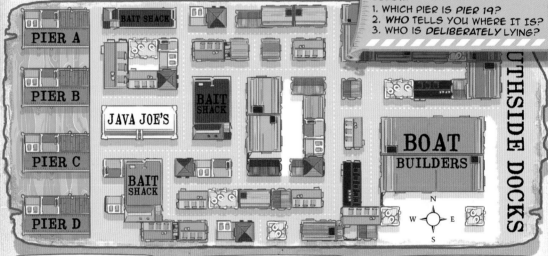

PIER A, PIER B, JAVA JOE'S, BAIT SHACK, PIER C, BAIT SHACK, PIER D, BOAT BUILDERS, SOUTHSIDE DOCKS

START BY FACING *NORTH* ON THE ROAD AT THE ... ER ... *SOUTH-WEST* CORNER OF THE *BOAT BUILDERS*, NEXT TO THE *RED BUILDING*. DRIVE ALONG THAT ROAD UNTIL YOU CAN GO NO FURTHER, THEN TURN ... UM ... *WEST*. CONTINUE WEST AND TAKE THE TURNING TO THE SOUTH *DIRECTLY* BEFORE A REALLY OLD BUILDING, I THINK IT'S CALLED THE *BAIT SHACK*. TAKE THE *SECOND* EXIT TO THE WEST OFF THIS ROAD AND CONTINUE ALONG UNTIL YOU REACH A *T-JUNCTION*. GO *SOUTH* AND FOLLOW THE ROAD ROUND TO THE *EAST*. AT THE END OF THIS ROAD IS PIER 19, I THINK!

PIER 19, EH? WELL, I'VE NEVER BEEN TO THE DOCKS, BUT I THINK I KNOW WHERE IT IS. START BY FACING *WEST* ON THE ROAD TO THE *NORTH* OF THE BOAT BUILDERS, NEXT TO THE RED BUILDING. DRIVE UNTIL YOU GET TO A *T-JUNCTION*. TURN *SOUTH* AND THEN TAKE THE *FIRST* TURNING TO THE *WEST*. KEEP GOING UNTIL YOU REACH THE BAIT SHACK, THEN TURN *NORTH*. TURN *WEST* AT THE FIRST OPPORTUNITY. GO PAST *JAVA JOE'S* – WHO INCIDENTALLY SERVE THE TASTIEST DOUGHNUTS I'VE EVER HAD – AND PIER 19 WILL BE RIGHT IN FRONT OF YOU.

LOST, HUH? WELL, THE BEST WAY TO GO IS TO START IN THE MIDDLE OF THE *CROSSROADS* AT THE *NORTH-WEST* CORNER OF THE *BOAT BUILDERS*. DRIVE IN THE DIRECTION OF THE NEAREST *GREEN* BUILDING. WHEN YOU GET TO IT TURN ... *NORTH* ... I THINK. AT THE NEXT *CROSSROADS* GO *WEST*. IF MY MEMORY SERVES THIS ROAD WILL TAKE YOU PAST A *BAIT SHACK*. IT *MIGHT* HAVE A RED ROOF, BUT I'M *NOT* SURE. TURN *SOUTH* AFTER THE BAIT SHACK AND THEN TAKE THE NEXT TURNING *WEST*. AT THE END OF THIS ROAD IS PIER 19.

 BARNEY BARNACLES
 ARNOLD ANCHORCHAIN
   RICK RIGGING

ADVENTURE PROGRESS *11%*

THE TELLTALE CELL

THE BOMBZILLA TEARS DOWN THE CREAKING JETTY AND SCREECHES TO A HALT OUTSIDE AN *OLD WOODEN SHACK*. VON DOOGAN LEAPS FROM THE VEHICLE AND RUNS TO THE DOOR, FUMBLING WITH THE *KEY* JAKE SENT HIM. THE PADLOCK DROPS, AND DOOGAN IS *IN*, BUT – HE'S *TOO LATE!* IT SEEMS THAT MERE *MOMENTS* BEFORE THE DOOG'S ARRIVAL, JAKE'S CAPTORS MOVED HIM *ELSEWHERE!*

DULL ISLAND   SCABB ISLAND   KOKOVOKO ISLAND
MONSTERA ISLAND   ONI WU ISLAND   MELEE ISLAND
SKULL ISLAND   TREASURE ISLAND   JAVASU ISLAND

N

RILORA   Sails only on:
Mondays in September
Wednesdays in November
Fridays in December

RAMONA   Sails only on:
Wednesdays in September
Fridays in November
Mondays in December

RALOMA   Sails only on:
Fridays in September
Mondays in November
Wednesdays in December

MAP
END
N
START:
OUR ROUTE

PROPERTY OF C.N.

EMBER
3 4 5 6
10 11 12
16 17...

Buy Milk
Saturday 6th

The ROOM

LOCATION A

LOCATION B

LOCATION C

LOCATION D

CAPTAINS ON DUTY TODAY:
– DIGBY –
– GUMP –
– NEMO –

The DOCKS

THERE ARE SEVERAL *CLUES* IN THE *ROOM*, AND OUT ON THE *DOCKS*. LOOKING *CAREFULLY* AT ALL THE EVIDENCE, DOOGAN BEGINS TO GET THE FEELING THAT HIS FRIEND MAY STILL BE *VERY CLOSE BY...!*

THE CHALLENGE!

USING THE *CLUES* THAT ARE DOTTED ABOUT THE ROOM AND THE DOCKS, ANSWER THE FOLLOWING QUESTIONS:
1. WHERE IS JAKE?
2. WHO HAS KIDNAPPED HIM?
3. WHERE IS HE LIKELY TO BE GOING NEXT?

ADVENTURE PROGRESS *14%*

POKER FACE

IMPOSSIBILITY LEVEL:

WITH JAKE LOCATED, DOOGAN'S MIND BEGINS TO *WHIRR!*

THAT BOAT'S GUARDED LIKE IT WAS MADE OF *GOLD!* GETTING ON BOARD'S GOING TO BE TRICKY! *HANG ABOUT,* THERE GOES A MEMBER OF THE CREW NOW...

OUR HERO TAILS THE SAILOR TO A GLOOMY WATERFRONT BAR...

A CARD GAME! AND IT LOOKS LIKE THE STAKES ARE PRETTY HIGH! LET'S SEE IF THEY HAVE ROOM FOR ONE MORE PLAYER!

THE GAME INVOLVES A SET OF CARDS THAT HAVE EITHER A *GHOST SHIP,* A *SEA MONSTER,* A *STORM* OR A *PIRATE* ON THEM. EACH CARD CAN *"BEAT"* ONE OTHER CARD, AS SHOWN IN THE CHART AT THE BOTTOM.

DOOGAN JOINS THE GAME, AND BIDES HIS TIME UNTIL THE SAILOR BETS HIS *SHIP'S PASS* IN A *DESPERATE* ATTEMPT TO WIN BACK SOME OF HIS MONEY!

PLAYER 1

PLAYER 2

PLAYER 3

PLAYER 4

WHO BEATS WHO?

BEATS

BEATS

BEATS

BEATS

THE CHALLENGE!

IN ORDER TO WIN THE GAME, DOOGAN MUST SELECT *FOUR* CARDS BY TAKING *ONE* FROM *EACH* OF THE OTHER PLAYERS. THESE FOUR CARDS MUST BE ABLE TO "BEAT" ALL FOUR CARDS IN *EACH* OF THE OTHER PLAYERS' REMAINING HANDS.

WHICH FOUR CARDS SHOULD DOOGAN TAKE?

ADVENTURE PROGRESS *16%*

A KNOTTY PROBLEM

DOOGAN SNATCHES UP THE BOARDING PASS AND **BOLTS** OUT OF THE TAVERN. MOMENTS LATER, ON BOARD THE **RAMONA**, HE QUICKLY SLIPS **BELOW DECKS**. IN A DINGY CORRIDOR CLOSE TO THE ENGINE ROOM, OUR HERO PUSHES OPEN A DOOR AND FINALLY COMES FACE TO FACE WITH HIS **KIDNAPPED PAL!** SUDDENLY, HOWEVER, THE DOOR SWINGS SHUT AND LOCKS THEM IN!

CHALLENGE ONE!

JAKE HAS BEEN TIED UP USING **FIVE** DIFFERENT TYPES OF KNOT. DOOGAN DIGS INTO HIS BAG AND PULLS OUT HIS MOST **IMPORTANT** ADVENTURING POSSESSION – THE DANGER JOURNAL! USING HIS HANDY GUIDE BELOW, CAN YOU IDENTIFY ALL FIVE KNOTS USED TO RESTRAIN JAKE?

JAKE! WE'RE **BOTH** IN A JAM NOW!

GRANNY KNOT	DOUBLE CARRICK BEND?	
OVERHAND KNOT	FISHERMAN'S KNOT	
SHEET BEND	SHEEPSHANK	
FIGURE EIGHT KNOT	DOUBLE OVERHAND	HITCHING TIE
RUNNING KNOT	TILLER'S HITCH	HALF HITCH
SURGEON'S KNOT	FISHERMAN'S EYE	TIMBER HITCH
BOW KNOT	FIGURE EIGHT DOUBLE	

CHALLENGE TWO!

NOW THAT YOU'VE FOUND AND UNTIED THE FIVE KNOTS, JOT DOWN THE **FIRST** LETTER OF THE NAME OF **EACH** KNOT. THESE LETTERS, WHEN **REARRANGED**, SPELL A WORD WHICH WILL LEAD YOU TO **WHERE** THE KEY TO THE DOOR IS HIDDEN. IN WHICH OF THE **RED NUMBERED LOCATIONS** IS THE KEY?

ADVENTURE PROGRESS *19%*

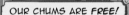

PUZZLE No. 8 — FINDING CAPTAIN NEMO

IMPOSSIBILITY LEVEL:

OUR CHUMS ARE *FREE!*

JAKE, YOU GO ASHORE AND ALERT THE AUTHORITIES — I'M GOING TO FIND THIS *CAPTAIN NEMO* CHARACTER!

RIGHT-O!

HOWEVER, SOON AFTERWARDS...

I'M LOST! THIS PLACE IS A LABYRINTH!

CHALLENGE ONE!

THE THREE IMAGES BELOW ARE SEEN THROUGH DOOGAN'S EYES. *ROOM A* IS THE ROOM DOOGAN IS IN, THE WALL BEHIND HIM HAS A *RED DOOR* ON IT. *ROOM B* IS THE VIEW THROUGH THE *LEFT* DOOR IN *ROOM A*. *ROOM C* IS THE VIEW THROUGH THE *RIGHT* DOOR IN *ROOM A*. USING THE BLUEPRINT OF THE B-DECK, CAN YOU FIGURE OUT *WHERE ROOM A IS?*

ROOM **A**

ROOM **B**

ROOM **C**

THE RAMONA

B-DECK

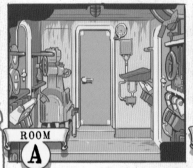

Captain's Cabin

KEY

ORANGE DOORS
GREEN DOORS
RED DOORS
PORTHOLES

CHALLENGE TWO!

DOOGAN HAS FOUND A *PHOTOGRAPH* OF THE *CAPTAIN'S CABIN*. LOOKING AT THE PHOTO ABOVE, AND THE BLUEPRINT, CAN YOU WORK OUT *WHERE THE CAPTAIN'S CABIN IS?*

CHALLENGE THREE!

NOW THAT YOU'VE FIGURED OUT WHERE DOOGAN *IS* AND WHERE HE'S *GOING*, HE NEEDS TO GET THERE *UNSEEN!* DOOGAN CAN GO THROUGH ANY DOORWAY EXCEPT *RED DOORS*, WHICH ARE ALL *LOCKED*. WHAT IS THE LEAST NUMBER OF PORTHOLES YOU CAN PASS, WHEN WALKING BETWEEN THE TWO LOCATIONS?

ADVENTURE PROGRESS 22%

SECRET SNAPSHOTS

IMPOSSIBILITY LEVEL:

HAVING FINALLY DISCOVERED THE IDENTITY OF *CAPTAIN NEMO*, DOOGAN GOES IN SEARCH OF HIM. SNEAKING UP ON DECK, HE DISCOVERS THE *SHIP'S CREW* ALL HARD AT WORK...

THE *RAMONA* MAY NOT BE A REGULAR *TRAWLER* AFTER ALL, BUT THE CREW'S STILL UP TO SOMETHING *FISHY!* PERHAPS MY *RED SNAPPER* CAN HELP ME LAND A *BIG CATCH!*

DOOGAN HAS A VERY SPECIAL CAMERA CALLED THE *RED SNAPPER*, WHICH ZOOMS IN ON *THREE* AREAS IN EACH PHOTO IT TAKES. HE NEEDS TO PHOTOGRAPH ALL *NINE* OF THE ITEMS IN THE LIST AT THE BOTTOM OF THE PAGE, BUT HE ONLY HAS ENOUGH FILM LEFT TO TAKE *THREE* PHOTOS. PRINT AND CUT OUT (OR TRACE AROUND) THE RED SNAPPER, READ THE *GUIDE* BELOW ON HOW TO USE IT, AND GET SHOOTING!

TO *COMPLETE THIS CHALLENGE* YOU'LL NEED TO GRAB THE *CAMERA* FROM

DOOGAN'S DANGER KIT

Quick! GO TO PAGE → 47

RED SNAPPER USER GUIDE

Once you have cut out or traced around the RED SNAPPER, cut out the four holes. To take a photograph the central view finder MUST be lined up over one of the NUMBERED WHITE SQUARES in the picture above. You can ROTATE the camera to take photos upside down or on its side, but the central view finder MUST ALWAYS be lined up over a white square to take a picture.

ANY OBJECTS THAT APPEAR IN THE THREE ZOOM WINDOWS WILL BE PHOTOGRAPHED.

THE CHALLENGE!

WHICH *THREE SQUARES* SHOULD DOOGAN LINE THE VIEW FINDER UP WITH TO PHOTOGRAPH ALL *NINE* OF THESE THINGS?

ADVENTURE PROGRESS 27%

THE CRATE ESCAPE

IMPOSSIBILITY LEVEL:

JUST AS DOOGAN SNAPS HIS LAST PICTURE...!

HEY, LADS! THERE'S SOMEONE HIDDEN BACK THERE TAKING *PHOTOGRAPHS!*

SPOTTED! AND WITH THE ODDS AT *EIGHT BRINY DECKHANDS* TO ONE VON DOOGAN, I'D BETTER MAKE A RUN FOR IT!

OUR HERO IS PURSUED DOWN TO THE SHIP'S HOLD...

A WALL OF CRATES! I'M TRAPPED!

DOOGAN MUST FIND THE **CORRECT ROUTE** OVER THE CRATES TO ONE OF THE PORTHOLES.

HE CAN PICK UP AND MOVE THE RED LADDERS TO AID HIS ESCAPE...!

THE RULES

UNLESS you have a LADDER you can ONLY climb UP or DOWN the side of a crate if it has BLUE STEP BARS.

You CANNOT cross any gap between crates UNLESS you have a long enough LADDER.

LADDERS can only be used if you are standing on a CRATE.

The ladders are VERY WEAK, and as soon as they have been used ONCE they FALL TO BITS behind you.

START

CHALLENGE ONE!

1. *WHICH PORTHOLE* CAN DOOGAN ESCAPE THROUGH?
2. WHAT IS THE *LEAST NUMBER OF LADDERS* NEEDED FOR HIS ESCAPE?

CHALLENGE TWO!

THERE IS A *SECRET MESSAGE* HIDDEN ON THE CRATES WHICH REVEALS THEIR *CONTENTS. WHAT DO THE CRATES CONTAIN?*

ADVENTURE PROGRESS 30%

THE BIG BLUFF

IMPOSSIBILITY LEVEL:

DOOGAN CLIMBS THROUGH THE PORTHOLE AND UP ON DECK, TO DISCOVER THAT THE *RAMONA* HAS *SET SAIL!* MOMENTARILY DISTRACTED, HE FAILS TO SPOT THE EVIL FIRST MATE, *MR SHACKLE*, APPROACHING! THE DOOG'S *ONLY HOPE* NOW IS TO CONVINCE THE SAILOR THAT *HE IS A MEMBER OF THE CREW!*

BEGIN AT *PANEL NUMBER ONE*. EACH TIME *MR SHACKLE* ASKS YOU A QUESTION, YOU MUST *CHOOSE* AN ANSWER, AND THEN GO TO WHICHEVER PANEL NUMBER IS BENEATH THAT ANSWER FOR THE NEXT QUESTION, AND SO ON. YOUR GOAL IS TO GET FROM PANEL ONE TO THE *"HOODWINKED!"* PANEL WITHOUT BEING DISCOVERED AS A SPY! BE CAREFUL, THE MORE *SUSPICIOUS* MR SHACKLE GETS, THE MORE HE JUMPS TO *CONCLUSIONS!*

THE CHALLENGE!

WHAT IS THE CORRECT BLUFFING PANEL ORDER?

ADVENTURE PROGRESS 32%

PUZZLE No.13

A CLANDESTINE CULINARY CRYPTOGRAM

IMPOSSIBILITY LEVEL:

MR SHACKLE LEAVES DOOGAN IN THE GALLEY, WHERE THE DOOG GETS BUSY LOOKING FOR *CLUES...*

> THERE'S MORE THAN JUST POTATOES COOKING ON THIS SHIP! SOMETHING TELLS ME THERE'S A *MESSAGE* HERE FROM *"NUMBER ELEVEN"*, IF ONLY I CAN FIND IT!

One Cheese pie and 2 Cream Buns!

2 Cheese pies and a Bowl of Chips.

Sausage and Mash and a Peanut Butter Pie.

Sausage and mash and a Cream Bun!

Sausage and Mash and a Bowl of Chips!

4 Cheese pie and 2 Cream Buns!

CHALLENGE ONE!

LOOK BELOW AT THE VARIOUS *ORDERS* FOR MEALS FROM THE CREW, AND THE *RECIPES* AND SPACES PROVIDED. USING THE *KEY* FOR HOW TO MAKE EACH MEAL. USING THE MUCH OF EACH INGREDIENT DOOGAN WILL NEED TO MAKE ALL THE MEALS.

RECIPES

CHEESE PIE:
4 CW • 4 F • 5 BP • 2 NUT • 2M

SAUSAGE AND MASH:
3 KOP • 6 S

CHIPS:
2 KOP

CREAM BUN:
2 F • 1BP • 3NUT • 1M

PEANUT BUTTER PIE:
2 NUT • 1M • 8CW

CHALLENGE ONE ANSWERS

DOOGAN NEEDS...

_____ Cheese Wheels
_____ Bags of Flour
_____ Packs of Butter
_____ Sausages
_____ *KILOS* of Potatoes
_____ Jars of Peanut Butter
_____ Pints of Milk

```
----- Key for recipes -----
CW = 1 Cheese Wheel.      F = 1 Bag of Flour
BP = 1 Butter Pack.       M = 1 Pint of Milk
KOP = 1 Kilo of Potatoes  S = 1 Sausage
NUT = 1 Jar of Peanut Butter.
```

CHALLENGE TWO!

LOOKING AT THE SHIP'S GALLEY, YOU CAN SEE HOW MUCH OF *EACH INGREDIENT* DOOGAN HAS TO HAND. USING THE SPACES PROVIDED BELOW, WRITE DOWN HOW MUCH *EXTRA* OF *EACH INGREDIENT* HE WILL NEED TO GET FROM THE STORES TO COMPLETE ALL THE ORDERS FROM CHALLENGE ONE.

CHALLENGE TWO ANSWERS

DOOGAN NEEDS...

_____ Cheese Wheels
_____ *BAGS* of Flour
_____ Packs of Butter
_____ Sausages
_____ *500g BAGS* of Potatoes
_____ Jars of Peanut Butter
_____ Pints of Milk

CHALLENGE THREE!

LOOKING AT YOUR ANSWERS TO CHALLENGES *ONE* AND *TWO*, YOU SHOULD NOW HAVE 14 NUMBERS. USING THE *CODE BREAKER* FROM DOOGAN'S *DANGER JOURNAL*, WRITE DOWN THE *MESSAGE* THEY SPELL OUT IN THE SPACE BELOW!

CODE BREAKER

"Each number refers to a letter in the alphabet. 26 = A, 25 = B, 24 = C, etc."

THE MESSAGE

DON'T WANT TO WRITE IN YOUR BOOK? USE A SCRAP OF PAPER!

ADVENTURE PROGRESS 35%

THE MISSING MONIKER

MIDNIGHT! THE DARK SWELLS OF THE ENDLESS OCEAN LAP AT THE SIDES OF THE MYSTERY SHIP, RAMONA! ON BOARD, VON DOOGAN IS HEADING FOR HIS RENDEZ-VOUS WITH "NUMBER ELEVEN"!

HELLO? HMM... NO ONE ABOUT. WHAT'S THIS ON THE TABLE - A NOTE AND SOME KIND OF CHEQUERBOARD!

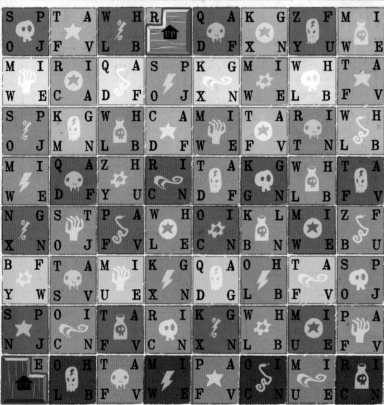

Doogan,

JAKE WINGNUT TOLD ME YOU WERE A GOOD CHAP, BUT I MUST BE SURE!

HERE, THEN, IS A PROBLEM THAT ONLY A TRUE PUZZLER CAN SOLVE.

* * * * *

THE CHALLENGE IS TO PLACE THE EIGHT WOODEN PIECES ON THE BOARD SO THAT NO TWO PIECES SHARE THE SAME ROW, COLUMN OR DIAGONAL. I'VE PUT THE FIRST TWO PIECES DOWN FOR YOU.

* * * * *

MAKE SURE THAT THE GREEN PIECE IS IN THE GREEN ROW, THE BLUE PIECE IS IN THE BLUE ROW, ETC.

* * * * *

ONCE YOU HAVE ALL THE PIECES IN THE CORRECT POSITIONS, THE LETTERS THAT SHOW THROUGH THE GAPS IN EACH PIECE (WHEN READ FROM TOP TO BOTTOM) WILL SPELL MY REAL NAME! SAY IT OUT LOUD AND I'LL COME OUT OF HIDING!

MAKE SURE THAT WHEN YOU PLACE THE PIECES ON THE BOARD THE ARROW ON EACH PIECE POINTS UP!

TO COMPLETE THIS CHALLENGE YOU'LL NEED TO GRAB THE PUZZLE PIECES FROM...

DOOGAN'S DANGER KIT

GO TO PAGE 47

THE CHALLENGE!

FOLLOW THE INSTRUCTIONS ON THE NOTE TO SOLVE THE PUZZLE - **WHAT IS NUMBER ELEVEN'S REAL NAME?**

ADVENTURE PROGRESS 38%

ROSTER RIDDLE

IMPOSSIBILITY LEVEL:

STANDING IN THE GLOOM OF CABIN B, DOOGAN TAKES A DEEP BREATH, AND SAYS THE NAME REVEALED BY THE BOARD OUT LOUD. ALMOST INSTANTLY THE LIGHTS COME ON AND *"NUMBER ELEVEN"* APPEARS. SWIFTLY, DOOGAN'S NEW FRIEND GETS DOWN TO BUSINESS...

THE CHALLENGE!

LOOKING AT THE *PAPERS* ON THE TABLE, FIGURE OUT A PATH THE DOOG CAN TAKE TO THE SAFE WITHOUT BEING SPOTTED. AT THE BOTTOM OF THE PAGE IS DOOGAN'S PLAN, BUT IT HAS SOME HOLES IN IT – CAN YOU FILL IN THE BLANKS?

ALL THE INFORMATION ABOUT THE SHIP'S VOYAGE IS HIDDEN IN A SAFE BELOW DECKS. IT'S 1:00AM *NOW*, AND THE SHIP IS DUE TO ARRIVE AT JAVASU ISLAND IN A FEW HOURS, SO WE MUST WORK *FAST* TO GET TO THE SAFE AND DISCOVER ITS *SECRETS!*

WATCHMEN "E" & "G"
Come on watch at 2:00am and take a ten-minute break **after 30 minutes.**

WATCHMAN "A"
On watch all night. Takes a ten-minute break at 1:15am and 2:00am.

WATCHMAN "B"
On duty from 1:00am to 2:00am only.

WATCHMAN "F"
On duty all night.

STAIRS TO C-DECK

B-Deck

WATCHMAN "H"
Comes on watch at 2:30am. Walks clockwise. Takes 10 minutes to walk each corridor.

WATCHMAN "C"
Comes on watch at 2:00am. Walks clockwise. Takes him 15 minutes to get halfway round his route.

C-Deck

SAFE

WATCHMAN "D"
Comes on watch at 2:15am. Takes 10 minutes before he has to turn around and walk back.

= STATIONARY WATCHMAN
= WALKING WATCHMAN.
= PATH OF WALKING WATCHMAN'S ROUTE.

SET OUT AT 1:15 AND RUN ROUND TO CORRIDOR 6 . STAY THERE UNTIL ABOUT 1:13 THEN RUN ALL THE WAY TO CORRIDOR 13 . HIDE THERE UNTIL ABOUT 1:15 , THEN RUN TO CORRIDOR 11 . WAIT THERE UNTIL 1:30 AND THEN RUN TO THE STAIRS AND HEAD DOWN TO C-DECK. ON C-DECK, HIDE IN CORRIDOR 16, AND WAIT UNTIL ABOUT 1:46 , THEN RUN TO THE SAFE ROOM.

ADVENTURE PROGRESS 40%

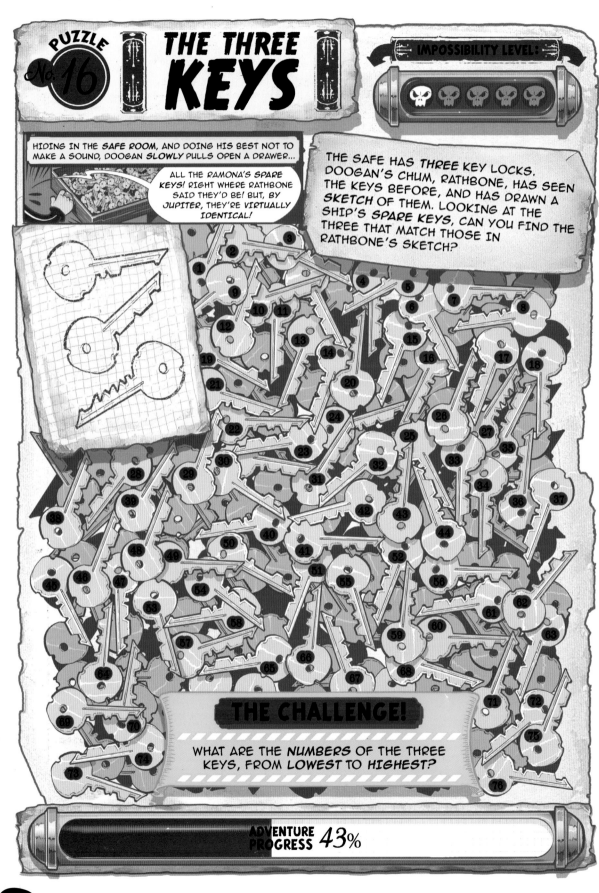

THE BIG PLUNGE

GATHERING UP THE *TOP SECRET DOCUMENTS* FROM THE SAFE, DOOGAN HEARS A CRY OF "*LAND HO!*". PEERING OUT OF A PORTHOLE, THE DOOG SEES THE FIRST LIGHT OF DAWN GLIMMERING FROM BEHIND THE OMINOUS SILHOUETTE OF *JAVASU ISLAND!* KNOWING HE HAS JUST *MOMENTS* BEFORE HIS THEFT IS DISCOVERED, OUR HERO IS ABOUT TO JUMP SHIP AND SWIM FOR SHORE WHEN RATHBONE SHOUTS TO HIM TO *STOP...!*

COOL YOUR JETS, *DOOG!* THESE WATERS ARE *LOUSY* WITH DANGER! MY COUSIN SID CAME THROUGH HERE *FIVE YEARS AGO*, AND HASN'T BEEN HEARD FROM SINCE! I'VE DRAWN A *MAP* OF THE BAY, AND THE *THREE* POSSIBLE ROUTES TO SHORE, PERHAPS *ONE* OF THEM WILL GET YOU THERE IN *ONE PIECE!*

START AT THE *RAMONA*. PICK A ROUTE TO TAKE AND SWIM IN THE DIRECTION MARKED BY THE ARROW (YOU MIGHT WANT TO USE A RULER TO HELP). CONTINUE UNTIL YOU GET TO A ROCK OR BARREL, ETC. YOU MUST THEN TURN AND SWIM IN THE DIRECTION OF THE ARROW ON THE NEW OBJECT, AND SO ON. IF THE ROUTE YOU'RE SWIMMING TAKES YOU *DIRECTLY* THROUGH A SHARK'S PATH IT'S CURTAINS FOR YOU!

Ramona
A B C

Safety!

THE CHALLENGE!

WHICH OF THE *THREE* ROUTES SHOULD DOOGAN TAKE TO REACH THE SHORE *SAFELY?*

ADVENTURE PROGRESS 46%

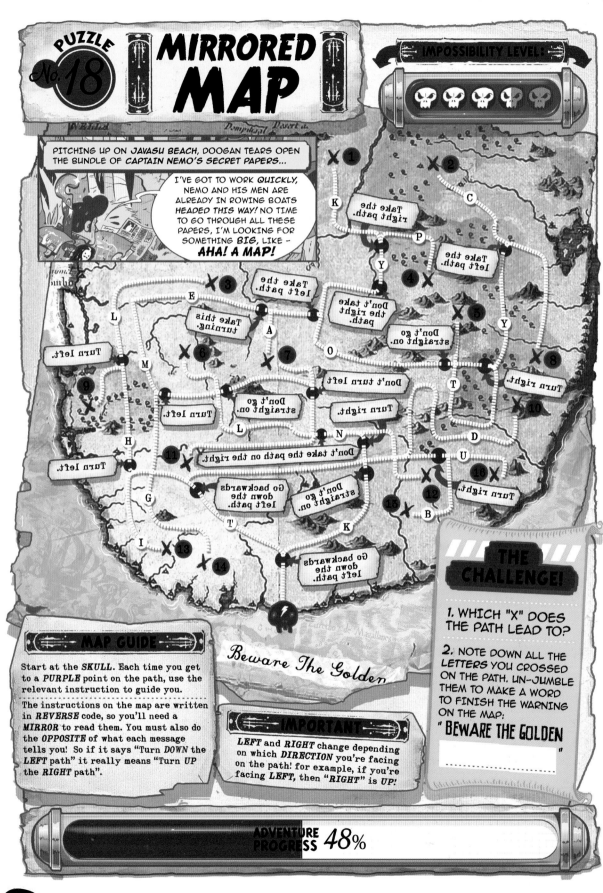

PUZZLE No. 18 — MIRRORED MAP

IMPOSSIBILITY LEVEL:

PITCHING UP ON *JAVASU BEACH*, DOOGAN TEARS OPEN THE BUNDLE OF *CAPTAIN NEMO'S SECRET PAPERS...*

I'VE GOT TO WORK *QUICKLY*, NEMO AND HIS MEN ARE ALREADY IN ROWING BOATS HEADED THIS WAY! NO TIME TO GO THROUGH ALL THESE PAPERS, I'M LOOKING FOR SOMETHING *BIG*, LIKE – *AHA! A MAP!*

MAP GUIDE

Start at the *SKULL*. Each time you get to a *PURPLE* point on the path, use the relevant instruction to guide you.

The instructions on the map are written in *REVERSE* code, so you'll need a *MIRROR* to read them. You must also do the *OPPOSITE* of what each message tells you! So if it says "Turn *DOWN* the *LEFT* path" it really means "Turn *UP* the *RIGHT* path".

IMPORTANT

LEFT and *RIGHT* change depending on which *DIRECTION* you're facing on the path! for example, if you're facing *LEFT*, then "*RIGHT*" is *UP*!

Beware The Golden

THE CHALLENGE!

1. WHICH "X" DOES THE PATH LEAD TO?

2. NOTE DOWN ALL THE *LETTERS* YOU CROSSED ON THE PATH. UN-JUMBLE THEM TO MAKE A WORD TO FINISH THE WARNING ON THE MAP:

" BEWARE THE GOLDEN
..............................."

ADVENTURE PROGRESS *48%*

AN UNEXPECTED EDIFICE

IMPOSSIBILITY LEVEL:

WITH *SKULL BRIDGE* BEHIND HIM, DOOGAN ARRIVES AT THE LOCATION MARKED WITH AN "X" ON NEMO'S MAP...

A *BUILDING* – IN THE MIDDLE OF THE *JUNGLE!* THIS MUST BE NEMO'S *HANDIWORK*. PERHAPS THERE ARE SOME *CLUES* TO HIS PLAN *INSIDE*...

THOSE *PIRATES* AREN'T FAR BEHIND, IF I CAN JUST FIND THE *OFFICE* I MAY GET THE INFO I'M AFTER!

Office door location is based on how many times the letter "E" appears in the building's name:
Zero = Door B
Once = Door C
Twice = Door A
Thrice = Door D

THE CHALLENGE!

1. LOOK AT THE *BLUEPRINTS* IN DOOGAN'S *DANGER JOURNAL*. WHICH OF THE *FACTORY TYPES* HAS THE SAME *PIPE* AND *POWER BOX* CONFIGURATION AS NEMO'S?

2. WITH THE FACTORY IDENTIFIED, CAN YOU FIGURE OUT *WHICH DOOR* LEADS TO THE *OFFICE?*

CANNING FACTORY

POWER STATION

SMELTING & CASTING PLANT

CHEMICAL PLANT

AEROPLANE BUILDERS

ADVENTURE PROGRESS 54%

THE BIG DISCOVERY

IMPOSSIBILITY LEVEL:

DARTING INTO THE OFFICE, DOOGAN SEES A LARGE DESK COVERED IN *NEWSPAPER CUTTINGS*. LAYING OUT THE *STOLEN PAPERS* FROM THE RAMONA ALONGSIDE THEM, DOOGAN FINALLY UNDERSTANDS JUST WHAT NEMO IS UP TO!

TOP SECRET

MISSING

RECENT EXPEDITION TO Javasu island left many ...he crew missing after ..." There was something ...er the ground. Some un- ...horror, a terrible sound."

POLICE SUSPICIONS

Some have blamed the master criminal, fro... Arsene Lupin, but Bart Wily has also b...

...returned to find the devasta...ion. ...was "totally shocked. I was away on busin... ...e owner, Bart Wily Bluff told reporters th... ...to use of the Deluxe Auction House or ...green, ...of which is said to be irreplaceable. ...s weekend resulted in a reported quar...

QUARTER OF A MILLION WORTH OF GOLD STOLEN

...BBERY OF AN EMINENT AUCTION HOUSE

Dear Sir, following your enquiry, I can confirm that Javasu Island is the only place where the minerals exist. To combine them with other metals you will need to physically BE on the island. Though why you would want to do this I cannot imagine.

POSTAL TELEGRAPH COMMERCIAL CABLES **TELEGRAM**

AT YOUR INSISTENCE I HAVE CONFIRMED THE ITEMS ARE GENUINE. I HOPE THIS NOW CONCLUDES OUR BUSINESS.

E.W.B.

The curious legend of the famous
LOST GOLDEN MONKEY

THE LAST TIME THE EX? visited the remote isl... he was told a story abou... golden monkey. The mon... said to be hidden in the... set on top of a stone bas... This engraving shows the... based on descriptions fro... natives of the island. Fol... scholars have claimed tha... due to its rarity and fame... worth two million pounds... The gold on the island has... rare minerals which don't... exist anywhere else.

There is a native legend th... golden monkey holds the ke... ancient creature, which wil... wake if the monkey is struck... lightning. The...

...CURSE HAS BEEN AROUND... ...many years. The sailors ...rted a terrible storm in ...enter of the island just ...minutes before the ...caused the ship to ..." Was like a huge ...derwater creature ...ole in the hull ...nything like it."

lightning has been recorded to contain 15 million volts of electricity

1 TESLA COIL GIVES OUT 15 MILLION VOLTS

To combine the gold with the minerals the machine needs 10 Tesla Coils To generate enough power.

SOLD AT ...auction ...today a ...r of rare ...ztec coins ...described ...uthentic" ...e recently ...den monkey. ...may be more ...red soon.

apparently same island ...den monkey.

Tell him that unles... he verifies the coins have no alternative but... frame him for the burgla... of his own business.
C.N.

THE CHALLENGE!
STUDY THE PAPERS, THEN *FILL IN THE BLANKS!*

CAPTAIN NEMO COMMITTED A ROBBERY AT THE _____ FROM WHICH HE STOLE SEVERAL TONS OF _____. NEMO THEN BUILT A MACHINE WHICH COMBINED SOME OF HIS SWAG WITH RARE _____ FROM JAVASU ISLAND. HE TURNED THIS NEW MATERIAL INTO _____ WHICH WERE VERIFIED AS GENUINE BY _____ WHOM NEMO WAS BLACKMAILING. THE CAPTAIN INTENDS TO USE THE REST OF HIS HAUL TO CREATE A FAKE OF THE FAMOUS LOST _____ AND TO SELL IT FOR _____ TIMES THE VALUE OF THE ORIGINAL ROBBERY. THE TEN _____ WHICH POWER NEMO'S MACHINE ARE AS POWERFUL AS A BOLT OF _____. DOOGAN THINKS THIS MAY HAVE UNINTENDED CONSEQUENCES...

ADVENTURE PROGRESS 56%

THREE STRIKES

IMPOSSIBILITY LEVEL:

RATHBONE'S REPLY HAS CONFIRMED DOOGAN'S *WORST FEARS...!*

THAT SMELTING MACHINE HAS TO BE *DESTROYED*, OR WE'RE ALL GOING TO FIND OURSELVES IN A VERY *NASTY* KIND OF *SOUP!*

SUDDENLY...

BANG! BANG! BANG!

THE *CREW!* THEY'RE *HERE*, AND THEY'RE TRYING TO *BREAK* THE DOOR DOWN!

NEMO HAS SOME KIND OF *SAFEGUARD MACHINE* IN PLACE TO COVER HIS TRACKS. IF I'M *QUICK* I MIGHT BE ABLE TO USE IT TO MY *OWN BENEFIT!*

MOTOR START

1 TON

SMELTING MACHINE

THE CHALLENGE!

THREE OF THE *GRENADES* DOOGAN FOUND WERE *DUDS*, BUT THEY MIGHT BE *HEAVY* ENOUGH TO HELP IN HIS PREDICAMENT IF THROWN IN THE *RIGHT DIRECTIONS*. WHAT ARE THE COORDINATES OF THE *THREE TARGETS* DOOGAN SHOULD AIM FOR?

1. TO BLOCK THE CREW:

X =   Y =

2. TO DISABLE THE MACHINE:

X =   Y =

3. TO OPEN THE ESCAPE HATCH:

X =   Y =

ESCAPE HATCH

MAIN ENTRANCE

Y AXIS

X AXIS

A   B   C   D   E   F   G

ADVENTURE PROGRESS 62%

THE JUNGLE HUNT

IMPOSSIBILITY LEVEL:

DOOGAN **BOLTS** OUT OF THE ESCAPE TUNNEL AND INTO THE JUNGLE, KNOWING HE MUST REACH SHORE, AND THE **RAMONA**, BEFORE THE CAPTAIN AND HIS MEN CATCH HIM...!

THE RULES

A) Print and cut out the four playing pieces. These represent three groups of Nemo's men, and Doogan. Alternatively, you can use coins, but be sure to mark one as THE DOOG!

B) Place DOOGAN on the spot marked with a GREEN "X" and the three NEMO pieces on the RED "X"s.

C) Each turn you FIRST move the *DOOGAN* piece ONE SPACE, and then you move *ALL THREE* NEMO pieces ONE SPACE, obeying the rules below:

1) YOU choose the path DOOGAN takes, BUT he can ONLY move *STRAIGHT UPWARDS* or *SIDEWAYS*, and he CANNOT use the same space twice!

2) The NEMO pieces ALWAYS move to the next space indicated by a BLUE ARROW. If one NEMO piece is blocking the path of another NEMO piece, the piece blocking the space moves FIRST.

DOOGAN IS CAUGHT **IF...**
He moves into a space occupied by one of Nemo's pieces, OR one of Nemo's pieces moves into a space occupied by Doogan!

SAFE! A
SAFE! B
SAFE! C
SAFE! D
SAFE! E
SAFE! F

X

X X X

GO TO PAGE 47

TO COMPLETE THIS CHALLENGE YOU'LL NEED THE PLAYING PIECES FROM...

DOOGAN'S DANGER KIT

THE CHALLENGE!

WHICH IS THE *FIRST* "SAFE" SPACE DOOGAN CAN REACH?

ADVENTURE PROGRESS 64%

THE GOLDEN MONKEY

WITH NEMO AND HIS MEN OUTWITTED, DOOGAN STOPS TO CATCH HIS BREATH. ABOVE THE CANOPY OF TREES, DARK STORM CLOUDS GATHER *OMINOUSLY.* DOOGAN IS JUST ABOUT TO SET OFF AGAIN, WHEN A TERRIBLE *SHUDDER* SHAKES THE GROUND APART *BENEATH HIS FEET...!*

YURGH!!

THE DOOG TUMBLES DOWN... *DOWN... DOWN!*

OOF! WHAT HAVE I LANDED ON?! FEELS LIKE A PILE OF *SCRAP METAL!* BETTER GET MY DANGER TORCH OUT...

DOOGAN GASPS – HAS HE DISCOVERED THE *REAL GOLDEN MONKEY?!*

GOLDEN MONKEY

HEAD
BODY
SHOULDER A
ARM A
HAND A
LEG A
FOOT A
FOOT B

NECK
CUBE
SHOULDER B
ARM B
HAND B
LEG B

THE CHALLENGE!

USING THE *PICTURE* OF THE GOLDEN MONKEY FROM DOOGAN'S *DANGER JOURNAL,* CAN YOU IDENTIFY THE *GENUINE* PIECES?

HEAD:	NECK:	SHOULDER A:	ARM A:	HAND A:	LEG A:	FOOT A:
BODY:	CUBE:	SHOULDER B:	ARM B:	HAND B:	LEG B:	FOOT B:

ADVENTURE PROGRESS 67%

LIGHTNING STRIKES

IMPOSSIBILITY LEVEL:

WITH HIS DANGER TORCH IN ONE HAND, AND THE *GOLDEN MONKEY* IN THE OTHER, DOOGAN BEGINS TO FEEL HIS WAY ALONG THE COLD, WET TUNNEL WALLS...

CATACOMBS! THEY MUST DATE BACK TO THE TIME OF THE *ANCIENTS!* AH! THERE'S A CRACK OF *LIGHT* UP AHEAD!

HOT SUGAR! I'M IN A *HUGE CRATER!* THE ONLY WAY ACROSS IS OVER THOSE *STONE* AND *METAL COLUMNS!* AND THERE'S A *LIGHTNING STORM* BREWING TOO, BY THE LOOKS OF THINGS!

THE *METAL COLUMNS* MAKE DOOGAN *MORE CONDUCTIVE TO LIGHTNING!* HE CAN TREAD ON *TWO* OF THESE WITHOUT GETTING *ZAPPED*, BUT IF HE STEPS ON A *THIRD*, HE'S *STRUCK!*

THE RULES!

DOOGAN CAN *ONLY* MOVE TO A COLUMN THAT IS TOUCHING THE *FLAT SIDE* OF THE COLUMN HE IS ON:

HE *CANNOT* MOVE TO A COLUMN THAT IS ONLY TOUCHING THE *CORNER* OF THE COLUMN HE IS ON:

THE CHALLENGE!

IF LIGHTNING STRIKES *KUTHULLU WAKES!* CAN DOOGAN GET TO THE FINISH *WITHOUT* STEPPING ON *THREE* METAL COLUMNS?

IF YES, WHAT IS THE *LEAST* NUMBER OF METAL COLUMNS HE STANDS ON?

IF *NO*, HOW CLOSE TO THE FINISH CAN DOOGAN GET WHEN HE GETS STRUCK? WHAT IS THE COLUMN LETTER?

FINISH

START

ADVENTURE PROGRESS 70%

THE BIG CHOICE

CATASTROPHE! DESPITE HIS BEST EFFORTS, DOOGAN COULD NOT AVOID THE GOLDEN MONKEY STATUE BEING *STRUCK BY LIGHTNING!* A HORRIFIC RUMBLE FILLS THE AIR, THE GROUND BESIDE DOOGAN FALLS AWAY AND A *DEATHLY* VOICE SPEAKS FROM THE *BLACKENED DEPTHS* OF JAVASU ISLAND...!

SUB—CREATURE! KUTHULU THE *GOZERIAN,* KUTHULU THE *DESTRUCTOR,* THE TRAVELLER HAS COME! CHOOSE AND PERISH! *CHOOSE!* CHOOSE THE *FORM* OF THE DESTRUCTOR! PICK *ONE* OF THESE NUMBERS AND SEAL YOUR *FATE!*

7, 6, 9, 1, 8, 10.

FOR A MOMENT DOOGAN'S MIND *REELS,* THEN HE REALISES WHAT THE OMINOUS MESSAGE *MEANS!* HE HIMSELF MUST CHOOSE THE FORM OF THE CREATURE, *KUTHULU!* DOOGAN SEES A *GRID* OF TILES ON THE CANYON WALL, BENEATH WHICH ARE SOME *INSTRUCTIONS...*

CROSS OFF THE TILES THAT YOU LAND ON! (left margin)

CROSS OFF THE TILES THAT YOU LAND ON! (right margin)

O³	U¹	L³	N⁴	N⁵	D³	F¹	U³	•²	G³	H⁴	T³	M⁴	T⁵	F⁴
U⁴	K²	•²	C³	I¹	E³	I⁴	E⁵	L⁵	J²	S⁷	T³	A²	E³	F¹⁰
T⁹	F³	E²	D²	S³	K³	•⁴	•⁴	•²	E²	D⁵	N²	A³	A²	C⁴
E³	•²	S³	•³	P²	E⁴	Q⁴	G²	•³	N³	E⁴	L³	S³	L³	A²
A³	A²	H³	E⁴	E⁴	C²	•²	•³	•²	S⁴	T²	U³	N²	T⁸	E³
V⁵	R⁴	R²	E⁴	W³	H²	T³	•²	R⁵	T²	•²	X³	C⁴	E³	H⁵
T⁴	•³	L⁵	E³	V²	L⁵	B⁶	O³	E³	Z²	L⁵	•²	S³	S⁴	•²

CHOOSE *ONE* OF THE *NUMBERS* KUTHULU GIVES YOU. FIND THAT NUMBER ON THE *GRID.* WRITE DOWN THE *LETTER* THAT APPEARS ON THAT TILE. THE NUMBER AND ARROW DIRECTION ON THE TILE WILL DIRECT YOU TO THE NEXT TILE YOU MUST MOVE TO...

EXAMPLE: A⁵ = WRITE DOWN THE LETTER *"A",* THEN MOVE *FIVE* TILES TO THE *RIGHT.*

WRITE DOWN THE LETTER FROM THE *NEW* TILE YOU ARE ON, THEN MOVE *AGAIN* USING THE *NEW NUMBER AND ARROW* TO DIRECT YOU. CONTINUE AROUND THE GRID UNTIL YOU HAVE *FOUR* WORDS.

THE CHALLENGE!

1. WHAT ARE THE *FOUR THINGS* KUTHULU WILL BE MADE FROM?

2. NOTE DOWN THE *LETTERS & FULL STOPS* ON ANY YELLOW TILES THAT YOU DID *NOT* LAND ON, STARTING AT THE *BOTTOM RIGHT* AND RUNNING ALONG THE ROWS FROM *RIGHT* TO *LEFT* ONE ROW AT A TIME. WHAT DOES THE MESSAGE SAY?

ADVENTURE PROGRESS 72%

KUTHULU'S FIRST TASK: STRENGTH

IMPOSSIBILITY LEVEL:

FROM THE *UNTOLD DEPTHS* OF THE *JAVASU PIT*, THE *HULKING TERROR* OF *KUTHULU* TAKES SHAPE AND BEGINS TO EMERGE, LIKE A GREAT MOUNTAIN OF *EVIL!*

HOLD YOUR HORSES, DREADED *KUTHULU!* BEFORE YOU UNLEASH YOUR *WRATH* UPON THE WORLD, I, *VON DOOGAN*, VOLUNTEER TO UNDERTAKE *THE THREE CHALLENGES* AND SEND YOU BACK TO *ETERNAL SLUMBER!*

VERY WELL, *FOOLHARDY ADVENTURER!* THOUGH IF YOU *FAIL*, YOU WILL BE THE *FIRST* TO *PERISH!* WE SHALL BEGIN WITH A TEST OF YOUR *STRENGTH*: "LIFT THIS ROCK I RAISE WITH *EASE*, AND I'LL ACCEPT YOUR *EXPERTISE!*"

KUTHULU PLACES THE BOULDER ON A *SPECIAL SET OF SCALES.* DOOGAN MUST PUT ITEMS IN THE *CHUTE* UNTIL THE WEIGHT ON THE LEFT OF THE SCALES IS EQUAL TO THAT OF THE *BOULDER.*

DOOGAN WEIGHS 12 STONE.
BOULDER A WEIGHS 50 STONE.
ROCKS G AND J ARE EACH HALF THE WEIGHT OF ROCK H
ROCK H AND ROCK R ARE THE SAME WEIGHT
ROCK D AND ROCK N ARE EACH HALF THE WEIGHT OF ROCK J
ROCK C IS 1/4 OF DOOGAN'S WEIGHT
ROCKS B, E AND L ARE ALL THE SAME WEIGHT.
ROCK F IS EXACTLY HALF THE WEIGHT OF DOOGAN.
ROCKS M, K, O AND I ARE ALL THE SAME WEIGHT AS DOOGAN.
ROCK Q IS 2 STONE LIGHTER THAN DOOGAN.
ROCK P IS 2/3 DOOGAN'S WEIGHT.
ROCKS B, E AND L COMBINED ARE 3 STONE HEAVIER THAN DOOGAN.
ROCK R IS HALF THE WEIGHT OF ROCK P.
ONLY BLUE ROCKS CAN BE STACKED AND STOOD ON.

CHUTE

What Doogan can do with rocks of different weights:

0 – 6 STONE
Can be lifted over head.

7 – 8 STONE
Can be lifted to waist height

9 – 10 STONE
Can be pushed but not lifted

11+ STONE
Cannot be moved.

THE CHALLENGE!

1) Which 3 rocks should Doogan fit together to reach the chute?

2) Which rocks can Doogan lift over his head and drop in the chute?

3) How much do they weigh in total?

4) What else can Doogan use to tip the scales?

ADVENTURE PROGRESS 75%

KUTHULU'S SECOND TASK: TRICKERY

MY FIRST TASK TESTED JUST YOUR *MUSCLE*, BUT NEXT OUR *INTELLECTS* MUST *TUSSLE*, ON ME A *TRICK* YOU MUST NOW *PLAY*, OR HAVE TO FACE YOUR *JUDGEMENT DAY!*

A TRICK, EH? OKAY – I BET I CAN PREDICT THE *COMBINED* ANSWERS TO SEVERAL MATHS PROBLEMS, USING MY *MAGIC STAMPS*, WITHOUT SEEING ANY OF THE *NUMBERS* YOU ENTER AT THE BEGINNING!

THE CHALLENGE!

THIS TIME *YOU* MUST PLAY AS *KUTHULU!* WORK THROUGH THE PUZZLES *IN ORDER*, WRITING THE RELEVANT ANSWERS IN THE BOXES (OR ON A SCRAP OF PAPER) AS YOU GO!

PUZZLE One

3 7 6 9
8 5 2 4

PICK *ONE* OF THE NUMBERS ABOVE AND WRITE IT HERE:

NOW MULTIPLY THE NUMBER IN BOX *"A"* BY 9, WRITE IT HERE:

ADD THE TWO DIGITS IN BOX *"B"* TOGETHER (EXAMPLE: IF YOU'VE WRITTEN 24 IN BOX *"B"* THEN 2 + 4 = 6).

ADD 33 TO THE NUMBER IN BOX *"C"* AND WRITE IT HERE:

PUZZLE Two

4 8 1 5 7
2 6 3 9

PICK *TWO* OF THE NUMBERS ABOVE AND WRITE THEM HERE:

ADD THE *TWO* DIGITS IN BOX *"E"* TOGETHER (EXAMPLE: IF YOU'VE WRITTEN 75 IN BOX *"E"* THEN 7 + 5 = 12).

SUBTRACT THE NUMBER IN BOX *"F"* FROM THE NUMBER IN BOX *"E"*. ANSWER GOES HERE:

PUZZLE Three

2 5 8 6 9
4 1 7 3

PICK *THREE* OF THE NUMBERS ABOVE AND WRITE THEM HERE IN ORDER FROM HIGHEST TO LOWEST:

REVERSE THE NUMBER IN BOX *"H"* (EXAMPLE: 731 REVERSED WOULD BE 137). WRITE THE REVERSED NUMBER HERE:

SUBTRACT THE NUMBER IN BOX *"I"* FROM THE NUMBER IN BOX *"H"*. WRITE THE ANSWER HERE:

ADD THE THREE DIGITS IN BOX *"J"* TOGETHER. WRITE THE ANSWER IN HERE:

SUBTRACT 13 FROM THE NUMBER IN BOX *"K"*. WRITE THE

LOOKING AT THE *CODE STAMPS* DOOGAN HAS SPREAD OUT, FIND THE *NUMBERS* THAT YOU HAVE WRITTEN IN BOX *"D"*, BOX *"G"* AND BOX *"L"*. WRITE THE CODES FROM THEM IN THIS ORDER:

BOX D STAMP CODE	BOX G STAMP CODE	BOX L STAMP CODE

READ THE CODE *BACKWARDS*. WHAT DOES IT SAY?

15 LIKN, 77 WAGI, 23 FVOL, 30 NAGO, 38 MAH, 50 JIL, 90 UQI, 2 IBEU, 36 NAGO
54 NAGO, 61 BAL, 66 YIUOI, 84 LOP, 21 PAIMI, 31 ADV, 63 NAGO, 39 DIFO, 19 EPLO, 28 RIT, 40 YPL, 7 USO, 80 AMG
89 KKP, 8 LAB, 5 ODNOV, 20 ZYN, 3 IKM, 37 CSO, 49 VED, 78 BXA, 18 NAGO, 47 FLB, 60 GPOI, 65 HUW, 16 RMG
11 TIO, 79 YHGN, 64 UIU, 42 SNIW, 57 IIRTY, 48 OLOJH, 34 YE, 62 NAAIA, 55 MIOL, 14 UAV, 41 QUIW, 33 WEVDB, 81 NAGO, 26 EEO
22 IOZBA, 72 NAGO, 24 OEMI, 32 PAI, 46 SEE, 76 DIMI, 68 FPL, 52 GAWN, 59 XYLOI, 67 COLO
43 HIST, 17 KAL, 35 JOUIL, 27 NAGO, 10 LOSA, 44 ZOI, 70 BIA, 9 NAGO
29, 74, 13, 58, 25 XIO

ADVENTURE PROGRESS 78%

PUZZLE No. 30

KUTHULU'S THIRD TASK: AGILITY

TWO DOWN, *ONE* TO GO! THE *THIRD* OF KUTHULU'S TASKS WILL TEST VON DOOGAN'S CAT-LIKE AGILITY TO THE *LIMITS*! DOOGAN HAS *ONE* LIVE HAND GRENADE LEFT – IF HE CAN GET CLOSE ENOUGH TO DROP IT AT KUTHULU'S FEET, THE GROUND WILL GIVE WAY AND THE MONSTER WILL BE *BANISHED* BACK BENEATH THE ISLAND!

CHALLENGE ONE

DOOGAN MUST FIND THE *WEAK SPOT* ON THE CAVERN FLOOR AND LURE KUTHULU THERE, BUT JUST *WHICH SPOT* IS THE WEAKEST?

CHALLENGE TWO

RIGHT! WITH HIS *TARGET AREA* IN SIGHT, DOOGAN NEEDS TO GET AS *CLOSE* TO KUTHULU AS HE CAN *WITHOUT BEING SEEN*! USING KUTHULU'S *BLIND SPOTS* AND *CANYON ROCKS* AS COVER, WHICH *LOCATION* CAN DOOGAN REACH?

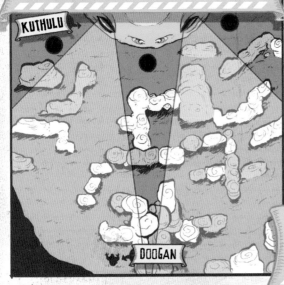

CHALLENGE THREE

DOOGAN MUST RUN THROUGH *FIRE* THAT KUTHULU HAS SET, AND DROP THE GRENADE! FOR EVERY *TWO* FLAMES DOOGAN JUMPS OVER HE MUST RUN THROUGH *ONE* PUDDLE TO EXTINGUISH HIS *SHOES*! WHICH *LOCATION* CAN HE REACH?

NINE VINE INCLINE

BOOM! THE GRENADE EXPLODES AND KUTHULU'S MASSIVE FORM *PLUNGES* INTO THE DARKNESS BELOW! THE DOOG IS KNOCKED OFF HIS FEET, AND THE PRECIOUS *GOLDEN MONKEY* SLIPS FROM HIS HANDS AND *FALLS IN* AFTER THE MONSTER! AS DOOGAN WATCHES, HE REALISES WITH *HORROR* THAT THE *ENTIRE CRATER* IS BEGINNING TO COLLAPSE IN ON ITSELF! HEARING A SHOUT, DOOGAN SEES A GROUP OF *NEMO'S MEN* AT THE TOP OF THE CRATER, THROWING VINES DOWN FOR HIM TO CLIMB UP!

THE CHALLENGE!

DOOGAN HAS SOME NOTES FROM *RATHBONE* ON A MEMBER OF THE CREW WHO MAY BE TRUSTWORTHY. USING THE *NOTES*, AND THE CREW *SNAPSHOTS* THAT WERE IN NEMO'S STOLEN PAPERS, ANSWER THE QUESTIONS BELOW:

1. WHICH CREW MEMBER IS *TRUSTWORTHY*?
2. HAS DOOGAN GRABBED THE *RIGHT VINE*?

FRUNK

VERNER

SHARKBAIT

BULL

CLAYTON

GOOSE

BUSTER

TUCKER

HUBERT

THE TRUSTWORTHY CREW MEMBER...

HAS NOT BEEN PHOTOGRAPHED ON THEIR OWN.

IS NOT IN A PICTURE WITH HUBERT.

HAS NEVER BEEN PICTURED IN THE MIDDLE OF A GROUP.

NEVER STANDS UNDER ANCHORS.

HAS NOT HAD TWO PHOTOS TAKEN WITH THE SAME PERSON.

VINE LABEL CODE BREAKER

USING THE SYSTEM THAT A=1, B=2, C=3 ETC. WORK OUT THE NUMBER OF A CREW MEMBER'S VINE BASED ON THE VALUE OF ALL THE LETTERS IN THEIR NAME ADDED TOGETHER.

ADVENTURE PROGRESS *83%*

DOUBLE TALK

IMPOSSIBILITY LEVEL:

AS DOOGAN REACHES THE CRATER LEDGE...

NEMO!

WE MEET AT LAST, *VON DOOGAN!* YOU HAVE BEEN THE *THORN* IN MY SIDE FOR TOO LONG, BUT NOW THE GLOVES ARE OFF AND THE *TWEEZERS* ARE IN MY HANDS!

ALTHOUGH DOOGAN KNOWS *BUSTER* IS TRUSTWORTHY, OUR HERO ISN'T SURE HE'LL *OPENLY ASSIST HIM*, WITH *NEMO* SO CLOSE BY. DOOGAN DECIDES TO FIND OUT FOR SURE IF BUSTER, OR *ANOTHER CREW MEMBER*, WILL HELP. WHILE NEMO *MONOLOGUES*, DOOGAN SPEAKS USING A *SPECIAL ADVENTURER'S CODE...*

IF YOU WANT TO AVOID *ANNIHILATION*, ANSWER THIS *INTERROGATION* WITHOUT *PREVARICATION*, OR THE *NEGOTIATION* WILL END IN YOUR *EXPIRATION!* SIMPLY PUT; TELL ME WHERE THE *GOLDEN MONKEY* IS, OR *DIE.*

I *WON'T* SPEAK! NOT TODAY, *CAPTAIN!* YOU THINK THE GOLDEN MONKEY SURVIVED? *UNLUCKY, NEMO!* FORGET THAT DREADED MONKEY GOLD!

A *LONG DROP* AND A *SHORT STOP*, THAT'S WHAT HE NEEDS!

YOU TELL 'IM BOSS!

YOU'RE TALKING *NONSENSE!* DON'T TRICK THE CAPTAIN! PUSH THE BLIGHTER IN! LET'S SEE HIM DODGE A *PLUMMET*, MATEYS!

OH, SUCH TOUGH TALK! YOU *CHUMPS!* DON'T THINK NEMO WILL ESCAPE NOW! RATHBONE HAS ALERTED A *BATTLESHIP!*

HE'S HIDDEN THAT MONKEY *SOMEWHERE!* I JUST *KNOW* IT!

GUMPINS

BULL

CPT. NEMO

HAMBONE

BUSTER

THE CHALLENGE!

USING THE CODE INSTRUCTIONS ANSWER THESE QUESTIONS:
1. *WHAT DOES DOOGAN ASK TO BE DONE?*
2. *WHO WILL HELP HIM?*
3. *WHAT SHOULD DOOGAN DO IN THE MEANTIME?*

- ADVENTURER'S CODE INSTRUCTIONS -

CODE WORDS ARE MADE OF THE *FIRST LETTER* OF EVERY WORD SPOKEN IN EACH *SENTENCE*. A NEW SENTENCE IS THE START OF A *NEW CODE WORD*. THE ALPHABETS ON THE RIGHT CAN THEN BE USED TO DECIPHER THE CODE WORDS.

DOOGAN WILL USE TWO OF THE ALPHABETS (ONE FOR EACH OF HIS SPEECH BUBBLES), AND HIS CONTACT WILL USE THE THIRD.

A	B	C	D	E	F	G	H	I	J	K	L	M	N	O	P	Q	R	S	T	U	V	W	X	Y	Z
R	Y	O	P	S	Z	T	U	X	V	Q	N	K	E	W	J	M	H	I	L	G	B	A	F	D	C

A	B	C	D	E	F	G	H	I	J	K	L	M	N	O	P	Q	R	S	T	U	V	W	X	Y	Z
Z	X	U	P	W	R	S	V	C	T	Q	K	E	Y	J	I	H	G	N	O	M	F	A	D	L	B

A	B	C	D	E	F	G	H	I	J	K	L	M	N	O	P	Q	R	S	T	U	V	W	X	Y	Z
I	M	P	K	B	D	Q	L	O	C	F	T	G	S	H	N	J	Z	A	E	X	W	R	V	Y	U

ADVENTURE PROGRESS 86%

SUCKER PUNCH

IMPOSSIBILITY LEVEL:

WITH THE SECRET HELP OF HIS NEW FRIEND, DOOGAN KNOWS THAT THE ELEMENT OF *SURPRISE* IS ON HIS SIDE, SO HE MUST STRIKE *QUICKLY!* HE THINKS THAT HE CAN *KNOCK OUT* ANY *ONE* MEMBER OF THE CREW WITH A WELL-TIMED SUDDEN *BOP* ON THE NOSE, BUT AFTER THAT HE COULD BE *OVERPOWERED BY THE REST!* HE MUST THEREFORE CAREFULLY CHOOSE *WHO* TO SLUG!

CREW MEMBER NAMES

1 = TUCKER 2 = GOOSE 3 = GUMPINS
4 = VERNER 5 = BUSTER 6 = HUBERT
7 = TUMBLER 8 = UNO 9 = SHARKBAIT
10 = FRUNK 11 = HAMBONE 12 = CLAYTON
13 = BULL 14 = KONK

CLAYTON WON'T FIGHT IF TUMBLER DOESN'T FIGHT. • BULL WON'T FIGHT IF GOOSE DOESN'T FIGHT • BUSTER WON'T FIGHT AS HE WANTS TO HELP DOOGAN. • VERNER WON'T FIGHT IF TUCKER DOESN'T FIGHT. • GOOSE WON'T FIGHT IF FRUNK DOESN'T FIGHT. • SHARKBAIT WON'T FIGHT IF VERNER DOESN'T FIGHT. • HAMBONE WON'T FIGHT AS HE WANTS TO HELP DOOGAN. • TUMBLER WON'T FIGHT IF GUMPINS DOESN'T FIGHT. • FRUNK WON'T FIGHT IF UNO DOESN'T FIGHT. • HUBERT WON'T FIGHT IF CLAYTON DOESN'T FIGHT. • GUMPINS WON'T FIGHT IF SHARKBAIT DOESN'T FIGHT. • KONK WON'T FIGHT IF HUBERT DOESN'T FIGHT. • TUCKER WON'T FIGHT IF BULL DOESN'T FIGHT.

THE CHALLENGE!

WHO SHOULD DOOGAN KNOCK OUT?

ADVENTURE PROGRESS 88%

RUMBLED IN THE JUNGLE

SOCK! ONE PUNCH, AND THE ENTIRE CREW **SURRENDERS**! SUDDENLY, A **VOICE** CALLS OUT FROM THE TREES...

DOOGAN!

JAKE! RATHBONE! REINFORCEMENTS AT LAST! HERE, GIVE ME A HAND WITH NEMO AND HIS MEN.

WELL, IT LOOKS LIKE THE GAME'S FINALLY UP FOR YOU, CAPTAIN! I – **HOT BANANAS! NEMO'S BOLTED!**

DOOG, RATHBONE AND JAKE CAN ALL SEE DIFFERENT PARTS OF THE JUNGLE. SPEAKING ON WALKIE-TALKIES, THEY *EACH* DESCRIBE NEMO'S MOVEMENTS AS HE RUNS IN AND OUT OF THEIR *RANGES OF VIEW*. LOOKING AT THE CLEARING, CAN YOU PLOT NEMO'S PATH ACROSS THE JUNGLE?

RATHBONE'S VIEW

DOOGAN'S VIEW

JAKE'S VIEW

JAKE HERE! I SAW NEMO ENTER THE AREA AT E1. HE RAN **STRAIGHT FORWARD** TO E2, THEN TURNED AND RAN TO A2. AFTER THAT I DIDN'T SEE HIM FOR A WHILE, THEN HE APPEARED AGAIN ALL THE WAY OVER IN H3. HE CREPT TOWARDS G3, AND THE LAST I SAW OF HIM HE WAS RIGHT THERE HIDING BEHIND A ROCK.

RATHBONE SPEAKING! THE FIRST I SAW OF OLD NEMO HE WAS RUNNING AT QUITE A **GALLOP** FROM A2 UP TO A5. HE THEN TURNED AND RAN IN A STRAIGHT LINE ACROSS THE ROCKS UP TO F5, WHICH IS WHERE I LOST SIGHT OF HIM. A LITTLE WHILE LATER HE RE-APPEARED IN F6, RAN TO D6, AND THE LAST I SAW OF HIM HE WAS RIGHT THERE HIDING BEHIND A TREE.

THE DOOG CHECKING IN! I FIRST SPOTTED NEMO RUNNING **TOWARDS** ME FROM F5. HE RAN ALL THE WAY TO I5, THEN CHANGED DIRECTION AND RAN TO H3. HE THEN SLOWED DOWN AND CREPT TO G3 WHERE HE HID BEHIND SOME ROCKS. HE MIGHT STILL BE THERE, BUT I HAVE A FEELING I SAW HIM A LITTLE WHILE LATER HEADING TOWARDS F6.

THE CHALLENGE!
IN WHICH SQUARE IS CAPTAIN NEMO HIDING?

ADVENTURE PROGRESS *91%*

THE GOLDEN CUBE

IMPOSSIBILITY LEVEL

DOOGAN *CHARGES* AFTER NEMO, AND IS JUST ABOUT TO GRAB HIM, WHEN OUR HERO TRIPS ON A *STONE SLAB* JUTTING FROM THE GROUND!

TRIP!

AT THAT INSTANT, A *GOLDEN CUBE* DROPS AT HIS FEET! PICKING IT UP, DOOGAN REALISES IT MUST BE A PART OF THE *GOLDEN MONKEY* THAT CAUGHT IN HIS *JACKET* WHEN THE STATUE FELL INTO THE CANYON. STILL ANGRY ABOUT LOSING NEMO, IT TAKES DOOGAN A MOMENT TO REALISE THAT *THE GOLDEN CUBE AND THE STONE SLAB MAY BE LINKED...!*

TO *COMPLETE THIS CHALLENGE* YOU'LL NEED TO BUILD THE *GOLDEN CUBE* FROM

DOOGAN'S DANGER KIT

Quick! GO TO PAGE **47**

OR ALTERNATIVELY, USE A 6-SIDED DICE.

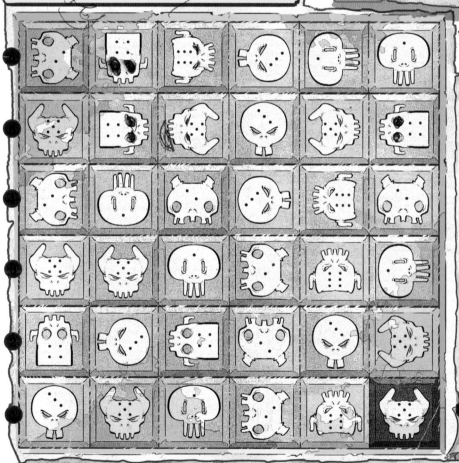

HOW TO PLAY:

1) PLACE THE CUBE ON THE *RED* SQUARE, SO THAT THE *TOP FACE* OF THE CUBE IS THE *SAME* AS THE SYMBOL ON THE SQUARE. IF YOU'RE USING A DICE, PLACE IT SO *NUMBER 5* IS ON *TOP*, AND *NUMBER 1* IS ON THE *LEFT FACE*.

2) TO MOVE, *TIP* THE CUBE ONTO A SQUARE *ABOVE, BELOW* OR *BESIDE* THE SQUARE YOU ARE ON. AS YOU *TIP* THE CUBE ONTO A NEW SQUARE, THE *NEW TOP FACE* OF THE CUBE *MUST MATCH* THAT OF THE SQUARE YOU'RE MOVING ONTO.

3) COMPLETE THE PUZZLE BY REACHING ONE OF THE SIX *NUMBERED SQUARES* ON THE *LEFT* OF THE SLAB.

THE CHALLENGE!

WHICH SQUARE CAN THE CUBE REACH?

FATE HAS FINALLY DEALT DOOGAN SOME *GOOD FORTUNE!* ROLLING THE *GOLD CUBE* OVER THE STRANGE *SLAB*, OUR HERO HEARS FROM BELOW THE CLANKS AND RUMBLES OF ANCIENT MACHINERY. TENSE MOMENTS PASS, THEN A HUGE BOULDER SILENTLY SHIFTS IN THE SAND TO REVEAL A CURIOUS HIDDEN *TREASURE CHAMBER!* AS THE DOOG STEPS INSIDE AN *UNEARTHLY VOICE* SPEAKS...!

CHOOSE WELL THE THINGS THAT YOU MOST *TREASURE*, FOR *GREED* IS MET WITH MY *DISPLEASURE*, TAKE JUST *THREE THINGS*, THEN LEAVE THIS *ROOM*, OR THESE *FOUR WALLS* SHALL BE YOUR *TOMB!*

It is thought that the values of items from Javasu are directly tied to how much gold is present in any one artefact. However, some experts claim a giant emerald of even greater value may exist on the island.

Javasu's soil also contains minerals from a piece of space debris from the great green Asteroid "X". A piece of this astral rock would be a rare treasure indeed.

The strangest treasures on the island are the carved idols of the god Kuthulu. This deity was said to choose its form based on the thoughts of whoever awoke it, and as such the idols discovered so far have taken many different forms. A true depiction of Kuthulu would be the most unusual of the carved idols.

While a wooden carving of Kuthulu would be the strangest item, it would not be the rarest. That honour would go to any idol carved from the asteroid rock, which turns a blueish hue over time.

THE CHALLENGE

STUDY THE *TREASURE CHAMBER* AND DOOGAN'S *CLIPPING* ABOUT *THE LOST TREASURES OF JAVASU*. YOU MUST HELP DOOGAN SELECT THE *RAREST* ITEM (FOR DONATING TO THE WORLD ADVENTURERS' CLUB MUSEUM), THE *STRANGEST* ITEM (FOR HIS OWN COLLECTION) AND THE *MOST VALUABLE* ITEM (TO SELL TO FUND HIS NEXT ADVENTURE!)...

RAREST: | STRANGEST: | MOST VALUABLE:

ADVENTURE PROGRESS 97%

THE LONG VOYAGE HOME

IMPOSSIBILITY LEVEL:

WITH THE ADVENTURE ON *JAVASU ISLAND* FINALLY WRAPPED UP, *VON DOOGAN, RATHBONE* AND *JAKE WINGNUT* SET SAIL WITH THE DASTARDLY CREW OF THE *RAMONA* UNDER THEIR WATCH. THREE DAYS LATER, AT THE PORT OF *KON-TIKI* THE CRIMINALS ARE HANDED OVER TO THE AUTHORITIES. THAT EVENING OUR THREE FRIENDS ARE PREPARING TO PART WAYS. RATHBONE IS HEADING NORTH TO THE FROZEN LANDS BEYOND *HERRINGBONE PASS*, JAKE HAS JUST RECEIVED *TOP SECRET* INSTRUCTIONS ABOUT A NEW AIRCRAFT HE IS TO TEST PILOT, AND THE DOOG IS LOOKING FORWARD TO THE LAST LEG OF HIS JOURNEY HOME.

DOOGAN! LOOK AT *THIS!* YOU MADE SOME GOOD INK, PAL!

THANKS, RATHBONE! IF ONLY THAT MEDDLESOME MARINER *NEMO* HADN'T SLIPPED THROUGH MY FINGERS!

WORLD ADVENTURERS'
Weekly CLUB *Digest*

Vol. 25 — No. 18 [NEW SERIES.]

RUMOURS OF *Secret* FLIGHT CHALLENGE - *See Page 8*

THE CURSE OF THE GOLDEN MONKEY

THE YOUNG ADVENTURER Von Doogan is today on his way home following a thrilling battle with the dangerous Cpt. Nemo on the hitherto uninhabited Javasu Island.

Having outwitted the Captain and his crew aboard the *Ramona* and then across the dangerous terrain of the jungle island, Doogan eventually lost sight of Nemo near a series of underwater caves, which pepper the south side of the island. A battleship, which had been waiting offshore, was observing a large whale in the water when they saw Doogan, Jake Wingnut and Rathbone in

RARE TREASURES

IT IS REPORTED THAT THE World Adventurers' Club is to receive a unique donation to its ever-growing collection in the form of a most impressive piece of ancient native art from Javasu Island. The item, which has been donated by Mr Doogan, is said to glow curiously at night, as many items from the island do, due to minerals present from a piece of the strange Asteroid "X".

UNUSUAL PHOSPHORESCENCE

SCIENTISTS AT THE H.B. research station reported a large build-up of a mystery undersea light-emitting substance. "As wide as a bus and longer than three or

JAVASU ISLAND LOCATION FINALLY REVEALED

MINERALS POWER SOURCE?

NEW RESEARCH POINTS to the possible use of asteroid minerals to fuel engines. "It could power a tank, a jet, or even a submarine" said

STRANGE CURRENTS

UNUSUAL UNDERWATER currents have been noted near Koko Voko

MORE SIGHTINGS OF "GIANT METAL MEN"

THE CHALLENGE!

1. WHAT DID NEMO USE TO ESCAPE?
2. IN WHICH DIRECTION IS HE HEADING?

ADVENTURE COMPLETED!

THE CLUES

PUZZLE
DOOGAN HAS FOUND A *SECOND* SET OF NOTES. PERHAPS THEY CAN HELP YOU FILL IN SOME OF THE BLANKS?

- THE NINTH LOCK TO BE UNLOCKED IS LOCK E
- THE SECOND LOCK TO BE UNLOCKED IS LOCK D
- THE SIXTH LOCK TO BE UNLOCKED IS LOCK C
- THE THIRD LOCK TO BE UNLOCKED IS LOCK G
- THE EIGHTH LOCK TO BE UNLOCKED IS LOCK A

PUZZLE
DOOGAN HAS SEEN THAT THE ALPHABET NOTE TELLS HIM WHICH SYMBOL REPRESENTS *"A"*, AND HAS FILLED IN THE REST OF THE LETTERS FROM THERE...

ANCIENT ALPHABET
Runs in clockwise direction

PUZZLE

LOOKING AROUND, DOOGAN SEES THAT *THIS IS* ONE OF THE ENGINE PARTS HE SHOULD USE.

PUZZLE
DOOGAN REALISES THAT IT'S *IMPOSSIBLE* TO EAT AT THE ESTABLISHMENT BELOW WITHOUT HAVING *EVER* BEEN TO THE DOCKS. HE ALSO DECIDES THAT *BARNEY* IS NEITHER *LYING*, NOR IS HE *RIGHT*.

JAVA JOE'S

PUZZLE
DOOGAN THINKS THAT JAKE IS ON WHICHEVER SHIP SAILS ON *FRIDAY 12TH NOVEMBER*. HE ALSO THINKS THE SHIP IS HEADED FOR THE *ISLAND ON THE LEFT*.

PUZZLE
DOOGAN TAKES THESE CARDS FROM *PLAYER 1* AND *PLAYER 4*:

PUZZLE

THESE ARE THE *FIVE KNOTS*.

PUZZLE
DOOGAN THINKS THAT ROOM *B* IS HERE:

HE ALSO THINKS THAT THE *CAPTAIN'S CABIN* IS SOMEWHERE AROUND THE *BOTTOM LEFT* OF THE BLUEPRINT...

PUZZLE TWO EXTRA NOTES:

Has a Furry Collar
Has a Red Hat

DOOGAN ALSO SEES SOME OF THE LETTERS IN THE NOTES ARE *RINGED*...

THE DOOG SEES THAT THE NINE ITEMS CAN BE PHOTOGRAPHED IN THESE GROUPS:

PHOTO *ONE*

PUZZLE

PHOTO *TWO*   **PHOTO *THREE***

DOOGAN STARTS BY FETCHING *THIS LADDER*:

PUZZLE AND USING IT TO CROSS THIS GAP:

PUZZLE
DOOGAN TRIES TELLING THE *TRUTH*!

PUZZLE
DOOGAN'S MADE SOME *NOTES*:

TOTAL INGREDIENTS *NEEDED*:
CHEESE WHEELS: 24
FLOUR BAGS: 26
BUTTER PACKS: 25
SAUSAGES: 18
KILOS OF POTATOES: 13
JARS OF PEANUT BUTTER: 25
PINTS OF MILK: 14

TOTAL INGREDIENTS IN GALLEY:
CHEESE WHEELS: 6
FLOUR BAGS: 3
BUTTER PACKS: 12
SAUSAGES: 0
500G BAGS OF POTATOES: 6
JARS OF PEANUT BUTTER: 6
PINTS OF MILK: 7

PUZZLE
HERE ARE TWO OF THE PIECES IN PLACE:

PUZZLE
HERE'S PART OF DOOGAN'S PLANNED ROUTE ACROSS *B-DECK*. THIS SHOULD HELP WITH FIGURING OUT THE *TIMINGS*...

Wait   Wait

DOOGAN FINDS THE *FIRST KEY* FAIRLY QUICKLY...

PUZZLE
...AND THE OTHER TWO ARE IN THE *RIGHT HAND SIDE* OF THE PILE.

PUZZLE
DOOGAN SEES IT'S DEFINITELY *NOT ROUTE A*.

PUZZLE No.78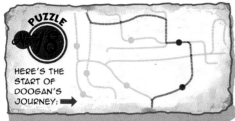

HERE'S THE START OF DOOGAN'S JOURNEY:→

PUZZLE No.79

DOOGAN HEADS OFF THIS WAY...→

PUZZLE No.80

IT'S DEFINITELY NOT THE *CANNING FACTORY, POWER STATION* OR *CHEMICAL PLANT*.

PUZZLE No.81

DOOGAN HAS MARKED SOME *DETAILS* THAT MAY GET YOU STARTED...↓

Tell him that unless he verifies the coins he has no alternative but frame him for the burglary of his own business. — C.N.

QUARTER OF A MILLION WORTH OF GOLD STOLEN

dBERY OF AN EMINENT AUCTION HOUSE a weekend is said to be irreplaced quar of which the Deluxe Auction House o e owner of the Deluxe Auction House ti treat. Earl Wily Bluff and reporters t was "Totally shocked. I was away on busin returned to find the devastation."

THE LAST TIME THE EX? visited the remote islan he was told a story about golden monkey. The monk said to be hidden in the set on top of a stone base This engraving shows the based on descriptions fron natives of the island. Fol scholars have claimed tha due to its rarity and fame worth two million pounds. The gold on the island has rare minerals which don't exist anywhere else.

PUZZLE No.82 THE MESSAGE BEGINS: "RATHBONE SPEAKING ON BOARD THE RAMONA..."

ONE GRENADE IS *HERE*: THE REST ARE AROUND THE *SPEECH BUBBLE*.→

PUZZLE No.83 TRY TRACING BACK FROM THE *SMELTING MACHINE, MAIN ENTRANCE* AND *ESCAPE HATCH* TO THE MOTORS THAT POWER THE SAFEGUARDS.

PUZZLE No.84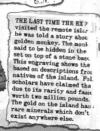

THESE ARE DOOGAN'S FIRST MOVES:→

PUZZLE No.85

DOOGAN FINDS SOME SMALL PARTS FIRST...→

PUZZLE No.86

DOOGAN CAN'T ACTUALLY WIN IN HERE, BUT HE CAN GET PRETTY CLOSE TO THE FINISH...

PUZZLE No.87

FOLLOWING THE RULES *CLOSELY* IS ALL YOU NEED TO DO TO SOLVE THIS ONE.

PUZZLE No.88 DOOGAN CAN LIFT ALL THE GREY ROCKS MARKED WITH A *TICK* OVER HIS HEAD.→

NOW, IF HE CAN SHIFT THOSE *BLUE ROCKS* INTO A *STAIRCASE*, THAT MIGHT HELP.

HE MIGHT EVEN BE ABLE TO GET INTO THE CHUTE HIMSELF...

PUZZLE No.89

CONCENTRATE ON YOUR *CALCULATIONS* AND THIS ONE WILL SOLVE ITSELF.

PUZZLE No.90

THIS AREA IS THE KEY TO SOLVING CHALLENGE ONE.→

PUZZLE No.91

DOOGAN HAS FOUND *THREE* MORE NOTES:→

- HAS A MOUSTACHE.
- IS ONLY IN TWO OF THE PHOTOGRAPHS.
- IS WEARING A HAT.

PUZZLE No.92 PERHAPS WHOEVER IS *CLOSEST* TO DOOGAN IS MOST LIKELY TO BE ABLE TO HELP?→

PUZZLE No.93

CREW MEMBER NAMES
- TUCKER
- GOOSE
- GUMPINS
- VERNER
- BUSTER
- HUBERT
- TUMBLER
- UNO
- SHARKBAIT
- FRUNK
- HAMBONE
- CLAYTON
- BULL
- KONK

THE LIST TELLS DOOGAN SOMETHING ABOUT THE INTENTIONS OF *THIRTEEN* MEMBERS OF THE CREW. THEREFORE, THE *ONE* CREW MEMBER WHO DOOGAN KNOWS LITTLE ABOUT IS THE ONE HE SHOULD *BOP*!

PUZZLE No.94

RATHBONE IS THE *LAST* PERSON TO SEE NEMO, SO HIS BROADCAST IS THE ONE TO *CONCENTRATE ON*!

PUZZLE No.95

HERE ARE DOOGAN'S *FIRST SIX* MOVES...

PUZZLE No.96

claim a giant emerald of even greater value may

A true depiction of Kuthulu would be the most unusual of the carved idols.

any idol carved from the asteroid rock, which turns a blueish hue over time.

THE DOOG HAS MARKED *THREE* DETAILS WHICH ARE IMPORTANT...

PUZZLE No.97 **THIS IS IT! AT LAST!**

THE *FINAL CHALLENGE*! AND YOU KNOW WHAT? I THINK YOU'VE GOT WHAT IT TAKES TO SOLVE THIS ONE *WITHOUT ANY HELP*!

THE SOLUTIONS

PUZZLE 1: THE NINE LOCKS

❶ DOOGAN FIRST WRITES DOWN THE POSITIONS OF LOCKS H, B, I AND F, SINCE THESE ARE DESCRIBED IN THE NOTES. WITH THESE FOUR IN PLACE, HE USES THE REST OF THE NOTES TO FIGURE OUT THE *FULL LOCK ORDER* AS FOLLOWS: F, D, G, B, I, C, H, A, E.
❷ TRACING THE WIRES IN THIS ORDER, HE GETS THE *CORRECT SWITCH SEQUENCE:*

7, 3, 2, 8, 9, 6, 1, 4, 5.

PUZZLE 3: ENGINE TROUBLE

THE ONLY ENGINE DOOGAN CAN FIND ALL THE PARTS FOR IS:

THE BIG BOPPER

PUZZLE 2: THE MYSTERIOUS PACKAGE

USING THE BLUE *ALPHABET NOTE* TO FIND THE LETTER "A" ON THE ANCIENT ALPHABET PAGE, DOOGAN DECODES THE ALPHABET, AND THEN DECIPHERS THE *LETTER*, WHICH READS:
"DEAR DOOGAN, JAKE HERE. AM TRAPPED AND YOU ARE MY ONLY HOPE OF ESCAPE. THE STAMPS IN THIS PACKAGE WILL TELL YOU WHERE I AM. ARRANGE THEM IN THE SAME ORDER AS THE STRIPES ON THE WOODEN PEG TO REVEAL THEIR MESSAGE. YOU WILL NEED TO BRING THE KEY WHICH IS HIDDEN IN THE STATUE WITH SIX TEETH AND A BROKEN EAR."
HE THEN ANSWERS THE QUESTIONS AS FOLLOWS:
❶ THE MESSAGE IS FROM JAKE, AND THE ENVELOPE'S SENDER IS J. WINGNUT, SO THE PACKAGE IS FROM JAKE WINGNUT.
❷ ARRANGING THE STAMPS IN THE *COLOUR ORDER* OF THE *STRIPES* ON THE PEG TELLS US JAKE IS AT
PIER 19 ON THE SOUTHSIDE DOCKS.
❸ THE KEY IS HIDDEN IN STATUE C.
❹ USING THE RUBBINGS AS REFERENCE, DOOGAN SEES THAT
THREE OF THE AZTEC COINS ARE FAKE.

PUZZLE 4: THE DISHONEST DIRECTIONS

❶ PIER 19 IS LABELLED *PIER B* ON THE MAP.

❷ RICK RIGGING TELLS YOU WHERE IT IS.
❸ ALTHOUGH BARNEY GIVES YOU THE WRONG DIRECTIONS (NOT EVEN ENDING AT A PIER!), THERE IS NOTHING IN HIS STATEMENT THAT IS OBVIOUSLY A LIE. ARNOLD ANCHORCHAIN IS THE ONE DELIBERATELY LYING, AS HE SAYS HE HAS NEVER BEEN TO THE DOCKS, AND YET ALSO SAYS THAT HE HAS EATEN AT JAVA JOE'S!

PUZZLE 6: POKER FACE

THE FOUR CARDS DOOGAN TAKES ARE:
PLAYER ❶ STORM   PLAYER ❷ GHOST SHIP
PLAYER ❸ SEA MONSTER
PLAYER ❹ GHOST SHIP

PUZZLE 5: THE TELLTALE CELL

❶ DOOGAN SEES ALL THE PAPERWORK AND MAPS RELATING TO A *VOYAGE*, AND DECIDES JAKE IS MOST LIKELY TO BE ON A BOAT IN THE DOCKS. THE TWO SCRAPS OF *CALENDAR* TELL HIM THE SHIP IS SAILING ON *NOVEMBER THE 12TH*. USING THE "BUY MILK" NOTE AND THE SAILING TIMES WALL CHART, DOOGAN SEES THAT THE 12TH OF NOVEMBER IS A FRIDAY, AND THE ONLY BOAT THAT SAILS ON A FRIDAY IN NOVEMBER IS THE RAMONA. BASED ON WHAT HE CAN SEE OF THE BOATS' NAMES, HE KNOWS THAT JAKE IS IN LOCATION B.
❷ LOOKING AT THE "CAPTAINS ON DUTY" SIGN AND THE "PROPERTY OF C.N." ON THE SIDE OF THE BOX IN THE ROOM, THE KIDNAPPER MUST BE CAPTAIN NEMO.
❸ THE ONLY ISLAND ON THE WALL CHART WHICH EXACTLY MATCHES THE ROUTE MAP IS JAVASU ISLAND.

PUZZLE 7: A KNOTTY PROBLEM

❶ THE FIVE KNOTS USED ARE:
A = OVERHAND KNOT   B = GRANNY KNOT
C = SURGEON'S KNOT   D = TIMBER HITCH
E = HALF HITCH
❷ REARRANGING THE FIRST LETTERS OF THE FIVE KNOTS, DOOGAN SPELLS THE WORD GHOST. THIS TELLS HIM THAT THE KEY IS IN LOCATION 4.

PUZZLE 9: SHIPMATES MIX-UP

❶ CAPTAIN NEMO IS IN PHOTO NUMBER 9
❷ DOOGAN SEES THAT JAKE HAS CIRCLED CERTAIN LETTERS IN THE NOTES. WHEN READ IN ORDER FROM TOP TO BOTTOM, THEY TELL US THE TRUSTWORTHY MEMBER OF THE CREW IS NUMBER ELEVEN.

PUZZLE 8: FINDING CAPTAIN NEMO

❶ BY LOOKING AT THE CONFIGURATION OF THE COLOURED DOORS, DOOGAN SEES THAT ROOM A IS ROOM 7 ON THE BLUEPRINT.
❷ THE ONLY ROOM WITH TWO PORTHOLES AND AN ORANGE DOOR IN THE CONFIGURATION OF THE CAPTAIN'S CABIN IS ROOM 21.
❸ THE LEAST NUMBER OF PORTHOLES DOOGAN CAN PASS IS SIX.

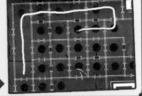

PUZZLE 10: SECRET SNAPSHOTS

DOOGAN LINES THE CAMERA UP WITH SQUARES
3, 7 AND 11
TO PHOTOGRAPH ALL NINE OF THE OBJECTS.

PUZZLE 11: THE CRATE ESCAPE

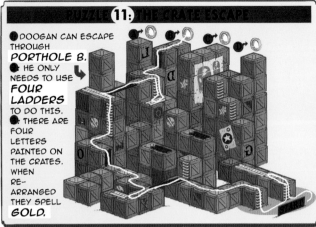

● DOOGAN CAN ESCAPE THROUGH **PORTHOLE B**.

● HE ONLY NEEDS TO USE **FOUR LADDERS** TO DO THIS.

●: THERE ARE FOUR LETTERS PAINTED ON THE CRATES. WHEN RE-ARRANGED THEY SPELL **GOLD**.

PUZZLE 12: THE BIG BLUFF

THE *CORRECT* BLUFFING ORDER IS:
1, 12, 5, 11, 6, 2, 10, 15, 14, 18.

PUZZLE 13: CULINARY CRYPTOGRAM

● DOOGAN NEEDS...
24 CHEESE WHEELS
26 BAGS OF FLOUR
25 BUTTER PACKS
18 SAUSAGES
13 KILOS OF POTATOES
25 JARS OF PEANUT BUTTER
14 PINTS OF MILK

●: DOOGAN WILL NEED TO GET...
18 CHEESE WHEELS
23 BAGS OF FLOUR
13 BUTTER PACKS
18 SAUSAGES
20 500G BAGS OF POTATOES
19 JARS OF PEANUT BUTTER
7 PINTS OF MILK

● THE MESSAGE READS:
"CABIN B MIDNIGHT"

PUZZLE 14: MISSING MONIKER

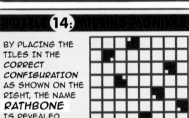

BY PLACING THE TILES IN THE *CORRECT CONFIGURATION* AS SHOWN ON THE RIGHT, THE NAME **RATHBONE** IS REVEALED.

PUZZLE 15: ROSTER RIDDLE

"SET OUT AT *2:00* AND RUN ROUND TO CORRIDOR *3*. STAY THERE UNTIL ABOUT *2:15* THEN RUN ALL THE WAY TO CORRIDOR *15*. HIDE THERE UNTIL ABOUT *2:25*, THEN RUN TO CORRIDOR *11*. WAIT THERE UNTIL *2:30* AND THEN RUN TO THE STAIRS AND HEAD DOWN TO C-DECK. ON C-DECK, HIDE IN CORRIDOR *16*, AND WAIT UNTIL ABOUT *2:50*, THEN RUN TO THE SAFE ROOM."

PUZZLE 16: THE THREE KEYS

THE THREE KEYS ARE:
27, 58 AND 63.

PUZZLE 17: THE BIG PLUNGE

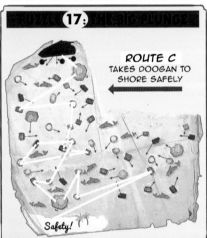

ROUTE C TAKES DOOGAN TO SHORE SAFELY

Safety!

PUZZLE 18: MIRRORED MAP

● DOOGAN'S PATH LEADS TO "X" **NUMBER 8**.

●: "BEWARE THE GOLDEN *MONKEY*"

PUZZLE 19: BOOBY-TRAP BRIDGE

THIS IS THE **SAFE ROUTE** ACROSS SKULL BRIDGE.

PUZZLE 20: UNEXPECTED WIRING

● DOOGAN SEES THAT THE BUILDING HAS THE SAME WIRING AS A **SMELTING & CASTING PLANT**.

● THE OFFICE IS **DOOR C**.

PUZZLE 21: THE BIG DISCOVERY

"CAPTAIN NEMO COMMITTED A ROBBERY AT THE *DELUXE AUCTION HOUSE* FROM WHICH HE STOLE SEVERAL TONS OF *GOLD*. NEMO THEN BUILT A MACHINE WHICH COMBINED SOME OF HIS SWAG WITH RARE *MINERALS* FROM JAVASU ISLAND. HE TURNED THIS NEW MATERIAL INTO *AZTEC COINS* WHICH WERE VERIFIED AS GENUINE BY *EARL WILY BLUFF* WHOM NEMO WAS BLACKMAILING. THE CAPTAIN INTENDS TO USE THE REST OF HIS HAUL TO CREATE A FAKE OF THE FAMOUS LOST *GOLDEN MONKEY* AND TO SELL IT FOR *EIGHT* TIMES THE VALUE OF THE ORIGINAL ROBBERY. THE TEN *TESLA COILS* WHICH POWER NEMO'S MACHINE ARE AS POWERFUL AS A BOLT OF *LIGHTNING*. DOOGAN THINKS THIS MAY HAVE UNINTENDED CONSEQUENCES..."

22:

● "RATHBONE SPEAKING ON BOARD THE RAMONA. WILL SEND MESSAGE ON TO JAKE WINGNUT ASKING FOR HELP. BEWARE THE CURSE OF THE GOLDEN MONKEY. IF CAPTAIN NEMO IS SUCCESSFUL HE MAY WAKE THE TERRIBLE ANCIENT BEAST KUTHULU THAT SLEEPS DEEP BELOW THE ISLAND. STOP HIM AT ALL COSTS."

● THERE ARE *FOUR* GRENADES.

23:

DOOGAN SHOULD THROW THE GRENADES AT THE MOTOR START BUTTONS FOR THE SMELTING MACHINE, MAIN ENTRANCE AND ESCAPE HATCH FAILSAFES. THESE ARE LOCATED AS FOLLOWS: **A3, F4 AND C6**

24:

THE FIRST SAFE SPACE DOOGAN CAN REACH IS C, AS SHOWN HERE.

25:

THE *GENUINE* PIECES OF THE GOLDEN MONKEY ARE AS FOLLOWS:
HEAD: **44**   NECK: **47**   SHOULDER A: **33**
ARM A: **4**   HAND A: **14**   LEG A: **60**
FOOT A: **49**   BODY: **17**   CUBE: **56**
SHOULDER B: **40**   ARM B: **12**   HAND B: **21**
LEG B: **7**   FOOT B: **63**

26:

DOOGAN CAN'T AVOID TREADING ON THREE METAL COLUMNS (SHOWN IN *WHITE*). THE CLOSEST HE CAN GET TO THE FINISH IS **COLUMN E.**

27:

1: THE FOUR THINGS KUTHULU WILL BE MADE FROM ARE:
BONE, SCALES, TENTACLES, AND *FIRE.*
2: THE CODE MESSAGE READS:
SOLVE. THE. THREE. CHALLENGES. AND. DEFEAT. KUTHULU

28:

● DOOGAN CAN PUSH ROCK *Q* UP AGAINST ROCK *O*, AND PLACE ROCK *P* BETWEEN THEM TO MAKE A STAIRCASE THAT WILL ALLOW HIM TO REACH THE CHUTE.
● *B, C, D, E, F, G, H, J, L, N* AND *R* ARE ALL LIGHT ENOUGH FOR DOOGAN TO LIFT *OVER HIS HEAD* AND INTO THE CHUTE.
● THE TOTAL WEIGHT OF THE ROCKS DOOGAN CAN GET IN THE CHUTE IS **38 STONE.**
● THE DOOG REALISES *HE CAN CLIMB IN THE CHUTE HIMSELF!* THIS WILL TAKE THE TOTAL WEIGHT TO EXACTLY **50 STONE!**

29:

THE MESSAGE READS:
VON DOOGAN WINS

30:

● *AREA 3* IS THE WEAKEST SPOT.

● DOOGAN CAN REACH **LOCATION B** WITHOUT BEING SEEN.

● DOOGAN CAN MAKE IT TO **LOCATION X.**

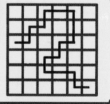

31:

1: *BUSTER* IS THE TRUSTWORTHY MEMBER OF THE CREW.
2: *NO*, DOOGAN HAS GRABBED ONE OF THE OTHER CREW MEMBER'S VINES!

32:

● DOOGAN FIRST USES THE *MIDDLE* ALPHABET, AND SAYS:
"CAN YOU LOOSEN MY ROPES?"
● HAMBONE THEN SPEAKS, USING THE *BOTTOM* ALPHABET, AND SAYS:
"YES, KEEP NEMO TALKING."
● DOOGAN SPEAKS AGAIN, USING THE *TOP* ALPHABET, AND SAYS:
"WILL DO. PLEASE HURRY!"

33:

DOOGAN KNOCKS OUT **NUMBER 8 – UNO.** IF *UNO* CAN'T FIGHT THEN *FRUNK* WON'T FIGHT. IF *FRUNK* WON'T FIGHT THEN *GOOSE* WON'T FIGHT, AND SO ON!

34:

NEMO IS HIDING BEHIND A TREE IN *D6.*

35:

THE CUBE CAN REACH **SQUARE FOUR** AS SHOWN ON THE RIGHT...

36:

DOOGAN CHOOSES...
RAREST ITEM: *P*
STRANGEST: *G*
MOST VALUABLE: *A*

37:

1: A *SUBMARINE* POWERED BY ISLAND ASTEROID MINERALS.
2: *NORTH-EAST* TOWARDS *KOKO VOKO.*

DOOGAN'S DANGER KIT

GET A FREE PRINTABLE DOWNLOAD OF DOOGAN'S KIT FROM THIS LINK:

WWW.THEPHOENIXCOMIC.CO.UK/DOOGAN

ALTERNATIVELY, *TRACE AROUND* THE ITEMS ON THIS PAGE.

PUZZLE
THE MISSING MONIKER

PUZZLE
SECRET SNAPSHOTS

PUZZLE
THE GOLDEN CUBE

PUZZLE
THE JUNGLE HUNT

This book is dedicated to Edward Doogan Etherington.

Little buddy, your own story has only just begun, but already I know it's going to be full of more adventure, fun and wonder than any tale I could ever dream up!

No matter how far you roam, or where your story takes you, I'll always be with you, full of pride in everything you do, cheering you on.

VON DOOGAN AND THE CURSE OF THE GOLDEN MONKEY

is a

DAVID FICKLING BOOK

First published in Great Britain in 2014 by
David Fickling Books,
31 Beaumont Street,
Oxford, OX1 2NP

www.davidficklingbooks.com

Text and illustrations © Lorenzo Etherington, 2014

978-1-910200-02-5

1 3 5 7 9 10 8 6 4 2

The right of Lorenzo Etherington to be identified as
the author and illustrator of this work has been asserted in
accordance with the Copyright, Designs and Patents Act 1988.

DAVID FICKLING BOOKS Reg. No. 8340307

A CIP catalogue record for this book is available from the British Library.

Printed and bound in Great Britain by Polestar Stones.

David Fickling Books supports the Forest Stewardship Council (FSC), the
leading international forest certification organisation. All our titles that
are printed on Greenpeace-approved FSC-certified paper carry the FSC logo.

MIX
Paper from
responsible sources
FSC® C015140

FSC
www.fsc.org